In Remembrance of Me

Enriching Our Understanding of the Lord's Supper

Andrew C. Fleming

DPI

DISCIPLESHIP
PUBLICATIONS
INTERNATIONAL

In Remembrance of Me
© 2002 by Discipleship Publications International
2 Sterling Road, Billerica, Mass. 01862-2595

Printed in the United States of America

ISBN: 1-57782-162-9

Cover Design: Jennifer Matienzo
Interior Design: Tony Bonazzi

To Jesus Christ, the only begotten Son of God,
who gives love definition, gives suffering purpose,
gives life meaning and who alone gives death potential—
such a book can be dedicated to none other

Contents

Acknowledgments

Thanks to the brothers and sisters of the Moscow Church of Christ, whose searching hearts and quest for truth brought this book into being. Thanks for the openness with which you embraced not only the message of Christ, but my family and me as well. Thanks for making our eight years of sojourn in your country seem like just a few moments and for making us feel completely at home in a distant land with a foreign culture and language. Not a day passes in which I do not thank God for your work produced by faith, labor prompted by love and endurance inspired by hope. With pride in my heart for you, I echo the words of Paul: "Even though you have ten thousand guardians in Christ, you do not have many fathers, for in Christ Jesus I became your father through the gospel" (1 Corinthians 4:15). We love you from the depths of our hearts!

Thanks to my beloved wife, Tammy, who has been my faithful partner in the gospel for more than fifteen years, through three languages and more than a dozen countries. Thanks for your joyful spirit, bright mind, constant smile and loving heart. Thanks for the balance you bring into my life and for reminding me of the joy of life when difficulties and problems dominate my attention. Thanks for sharing with me the joy of our two wonderful children—in you I have truly received what is good and favored from the Lord. You are truly more than I could have asked for or imagined. Thank you!

Thanks to all the great people at DPI, and especially to Kelly Petre for his patience and hard work. Thanks for taking the time to ask hard questions, make suggestions, read and then reread again. Thanks for all of your encouragement and spiritual insight—I have been enriched by the experience.

Thanks to our heavenly Father, who is the giver of all good gifts. Thank you for the incredible sacrifice of Jesus to whom we dedicate our lives. Thank you for eternal salvation and the hope of glory. Thanks for loving us first!

Introduction

On the evening of his betrayal almost two thousand years ago, a young, itinerant rabbi met in an upper room with his twelve closest disciples to observe the annual Passover celebration. Having begun his public ministry three years earlier, Jesus of Nazareth was now in Jerusalem, challenging the established norms and human authorities of the Jewish faith with his radical preaching and deep convictions. In preceding years he had traveled the countryside and spread his message to crowds of thousands who had gathered to hear his lessons; his underlying theme: "Repent, for the kingdom of heaven is near" (Matthew 4:17). Not only had his teaching awakened new hopes and dreams in the hearts of the people, but God had worked miracles by his hands, causing friend and foe alike to realize that an incredible power was at work among them.

With so much to tell, it is striking that the Gospel writers devote almost eight full chapters to recording the details of Jesus' final meal and time of fellowship with his disciples. This fact alone makes it clear that the evening's events were of the utmost significance and were meant to be understood by future generations. For that inner circle of disciples it would be an evening rich with fellowship and teaching that they would remember for the rest of their lives. It was during the observance of this particular Passover feast that Jesus dedicated a simple meal to himself, one that was to be commemorated by his disciples after his death. Making use of common elements that were within hands' reach on the table before him, Jesus set up this new memorial.

Although Jesus is not recorded as giving a name to the commemorative meal, Paul specifically referred to it as the "Lord's Supper." In time it has also come to be known as "communion," and the "Eucharist"— terms that will be further examined in the body of this book. With so many denominations teaching and practicing many different variations of this custom, it is both useful and unifying to simply go back to the New Testament to review the teaching found there about the Lord's Supper. The purpose of this book is to stimulate the hearts and minds of Christ's modern-day disciples to reflect more deeply on fulfilling one of our dying Lord's last requests: "Do this in remembrance of me" (Luke 22:19).

The Right Foundation

Two millennia is a long time when we measure it on the scale of human history. Not only can the specific facts about certain events become obscured with the passage of time, but the details of circumstance and intention that underlie these events can also become clouded and unclear. The process of recording history is not only prone to human error and sometimes even blatant corruption, but is also open to interpretation, since it is almost impossible for an observer *not* to be influenced by his own particular situation and context. Sadly, although the Greek New Testament boasts the most extensive manuscript attestation of the ancient world and is the undisputed basis of the Christian faith, Christianity is a religion known for its divisions and diversity of tradition and practice.

The first century church was "built on the foundation of the apostles and prophets, with Christ Jesus himself as the chief cornerstone" (Ephesians 2:20). Although some might therefore argue that the original church was built on men and the power of their personalities, it is more properly understood that the eternal truth of the teaching of these apostles and prophets, in perfect alignment with the teachings of Jesus, formed the foundation of the church. Their teaching was inspired by God's Spirit and empowered by their belief in the resurrection of Jesus Christ. The doctrinal unity of the first century church was dependent on its devotion to the apostles' teaching. Although these apostles and prophets have long since passed away, their legacy remains in the pages of the New Testament, just as God has ordained. Therefore the possibility of unity remains—the

Scriptures are able to provide today's church with the foundation it needs to be the "dwelling in which God lives by his Spirit" (Ephesians 2:22).

Hold to the Teaching

In seeking an explanation for the great variety of traditions that divide Christianity today, we should begin with Jesus' insights concerning the Jewish sects that divided the people of God in the first century. While archeology and history tell us that there were numerous divisions within first century Judaism— including Pharisees, Sadducees, Zealots and Essenes—the New Testament deals primarily with two of these factions: the Pharisees and the Sadducees. These groups differed greatly from each other in principle and practice, yet Jesus condemned both of them for incorrectly approaching and handling the Scriptures. Both factions were characterized by flawed assumptions as a result of their humanistic approach to faith in God and his inspired word:

- The Pharisees were so concerned with conforming to the traditions and practices that were passed down from preceding generations, that they replaced simple obedience to God's word with strict adherence to the teachings of men. Jesus condemned such misguided loyalty, for while it professed to honor God, it nonetheless emphasized man-made rules above God's laws (Matthew 15:7–9).
- The Sadducees believed that there was no resurrection (nor angels nor spirits, either) based on their confidence in the human ability to reason and to rationally deduct the truth. Jesus said very simply that they were in error because they did not know the Scriptures or the power of God (Matthew 22:23–32).

As we consider the diversity and divisions of present-day Christianity, it is clear that these same mistakes have been repeated with regard to the interpretation of New Testament teachings. The mind-sets represented by these two groups—whether following traditions based on what our predecessors have done or limiting the truth of Scripture to the confines of human reason—threaten both the unity and spiritual development of believers in our generation as well. When it comes to truly understanding the Lord's Supper, it is vital that we be willing to fight against these worldly patterns of thinking. The primary reason for embarking on this study is to deepen our understanding of the purpose behind Christ's commandment, and to share in the spiritual blessing that he intends for each participant to receive.

Jesus made it very clear that the surest way to know the truth is to believe his teaching and then put it into practice:

> To the Jews who had believed him, Jesus said, "If you hold to my teaching, you are really my disciples. Then you will know the truth, and the truth will set you free." (John 8:31–32)

Our approach to this study will be to consider the Biblical passages that pertain to the Lord's Supper in more or less chronological order. With the Gospel writers dedicating so much attention to this particular evening of our Lord's life, we are given a great opportunity to examine the setting in which Jesus chose to inaugurate the Lord's Supper and the immediate consequences in the lives of his disciples. We will begin by looking at the historical backdrop of the Passover celebration and how this significant Jewish feast gave the evening intrinsic meaning. We will examine both the Law of Moses and first century tradition to better understand Jesus' attitudes toward the customary celebration of Passover to help us determine how the celebration of the Lord's Supper should be passed on from generation to generation. We will then consider the experience of the disciples who spent this particular evening with Jesus. For them, it was a time of heightened emotion and expectation since Jesus had foretold the imminent coming of the kingdom of God and the inevitability of his own suffering, death and resurrection.

From there we will look at the practice of the early church as seen in the book of Acts and 1 Corinthians. Finally, we will consider some of the man-made traditions that have greatly affected the celebration of the Lord's Supper in later centuries.

Because our own understanding can be colored by years of traditional interpretation and individual experience, it is essential to reexamine the Lord's Supper in its original context to ensure that we are fulfilling God's purposes for its celebration today. Learning about some of the background issues that were relevant to the first partakers in the memorial meal will help us to deepen our own appreciation and practice. And as we review some of the pertinent passages, the origins of a number of our present-day traditions and practices will become clearer. Prayerfully, the pages that follow will lead to a richer understanding and experience of the Lord's Supper for all who seek to remember Jesus in the way he has commanded.

1

The Passover Celebration
Old Testament Background

For the inhabitants of first century Judea, the Passover celebration served as a reminder of a more glorious moment in their history: their redemption from bondage in Egypt. This memory must have weighed heavily on their hearts, since all around them were the proofs of an oppressive Roman occupation. Although they were fundamentally free to practice their religion according to the Law of Moses and the tradition of the elders, Roman regulation and taxation were imposed upon the routine of their daily lives. What longing must have filled the souls of God's chosen people as they collectively remembered the salvation of their forefathers by his mighty hand and the incredible dream of the promised land—the very place where they now lived as a conquered people under Roman rule. The Jewish nation was looking for a Messiah who would again usher in a kingdom like that of Solomon, and certainly many hoped that this Jesus, a descendant of David, might be just that one.

Significantly, Jesus chose to inaugurate his Supper in the context of one of the most important festivals of the Jewish year. A thorough review of the Old Testament teaching regarding the Passover is truly in order if we are to understand the setting and mind-set of those who shared the first Lord's Supper with Jesus on that fateful evening. You may find the going a bit slow in the next two chapters, but I encourage you to persevere. The information here will bring rich rewards.

Background History to the Passover

After Abraham obeyed God's call and left his people in Mesopotamia for the land that God would show him, he eventually settled in Canaan, the promised land. Abraham became the father of Isaac, who in turn became the father of Jacob. At the age of 130, Jacob, renamed "Israel" by God, together with his immediate family, migrated to Egypt because of a severe famine in the land of Canaan. Four hundred years later, this group of seventy had multiplied to about 600,000 men. Fearful of how powerful this nation had become in their midst, the Egyptians enslaved the Israelites and conscripted them into hard labor. God heard their cries and raised up for them a prophet, Moses, to lead them out of bondage. Before this time God was known as the God of Abraham, Isaac and Jacob—the God of *individuals* with whom he had made a covenant; but he was about to reveal himself as the God of Israel, the God of a *nation* in a covenant relationship.

Moses went to Pharaoh and asked for Israel's release, but Pharaoh arrogantly refused. Therefore, God demonstrated his miraculous power through a series of terrible plagues, but Pharaoh's heart remained hard. Finally God revealed to Moses that the last plague would be the most terrifying of all: the death of all the firstborn of Egypt, including people and livestock. To protect the people of Israel from this destruction, God instituted a sacrificial meal, the observance of which would save the firstborn of Israel from harm. This celebration was called the "Passover" because the destroying angel *passed over* the houses of Israel, thus sparing their firstborn. After the Israelites left Egypt, God wanted them to observe this feast annually as a reminder of the great deliverance that he had accomplished.

Although there are other references in Scripture to sacrifice and burnt offering that predate the Passover, the act of offering a single lamb in the place of the firstborn finds a parallel only in the story of the testing of Abraham's faith.[1] In circumstances reminiscent of the Passover, God had decreed that the firstborn son of promise, Isaac, should be sacrificed and put to death.

When he saw that Abraham had the faith to actually go through with such a sacrifice, God provided a ram caught in a nearby thicket to be sacrificed in the place of Isaac. Four centuries later, against this powerful backdrop of faith and deliverance, God called the descendants of Abraham to again demonstrate the faith of their ancestor—that the Almighty might bring about a similar salvation.

The First Passover Celebration

As recorded in Exodus 12:1–30, God gave Moses very specific instructions regarding the celebration of the Passover:

1) On the tenth day of the first month, each male head of a household was to select a year-old male lamb—either a sheep or a goat—without defect. Any household too small for a lamb was to share one with a neighboring household.

2) On the fourteenth day, the lambs were to be slaughtered at twilight, and blood from the sacrifice was to be spread on their doorposts and lintels. This would be a sign for the destroying angel to pass over that house.

3) The meat of this sacrifice—roasted, not raw or boiled—was to be eaten that same night, together with unleavened bread and bitter herbs. All the meat of the sacrificial lamb was either to be eaten or burned by sunrise.[2]

4) They were to eat in haste, with their cloaks tucked into their belts, sandals on their feet and staffs in hand.

5) The celebration was to be repeated annually and its meaning explained to the children.

6) The Passover began another celebration that lasted one week and was also to be devoted to God: the Feast of Unleavened Bread. During this week, no leaven (yeast) was to be found anywhere among the Israelites upon penalty of being cut off from the people, and on the first and last days of the week, no work was to be done except for food preparation. This was a practical reminder that

the Egyptians had urged the Israelites to leave with such haste that they did not have time to prepare their dough by adding yeast to it (Exodus 12:34, 39).

The very first Passover celebration was not a memorial, but an act of obedience and faithfulness whereby the firstborn of Israel were spared from the angel of death as the people prepared to flee their captivity in Egypt. Much of the detail of these Passover regulations focused on the selection, preparation and consumption of the sacrificial lamb, as well as the preparation for the exodus that was about to take place. The head of each household was to take full responsibility for making sure every detail was followed, and every household member was meant to participate. Even the children were to be instructed about the significance of the observance.

After witnessing the death of the firstborn of Egypt, Pharaoh finally let the Israelites go, as God commanded. The Israelites prepared to leave Egypt, but as they did so, other captive peoples decided to join them, either through faith or sheer opportunism. This made it necessary to add some further instructions to the observance of the Passover (Exodus 12:31–51):

7) No uncircumcised Israelite male could eat of the Passover.
8) No foreigner, sojourner, native of the land or hired servant should eat of it unless he had been circumcised.
9) None of the meat was to be taken outside the house.
10) None of the bones was to be broken.

The first two regulations that were added involved circumcision and were meant to remind the Israelites that their deliverance was not due to any particular quality they possessed or any personal covenant made with them; rather, they were delivered because of God's faithfulness to his promise to their forefather, Abraham. Circumcision was a sign for the descendants of Abraham that they were heirs of a promise that predated the Passover by more than four hundred years. The third amendment was probably introduced to ensure that the meat of the sacrifice was not treated profanely and that no other type of religious rite would be performed with it.[3] The meat was to be completely consumed by people or by fire before sunrise. (We will discuss the fourth new regulation in a subsequent section.)

The Second Passover Celebration

After Moses led the people out of Egypt, God very specifically instructed them about the way that they should live as his chosen people: separate and distinct from other nations. With these new laws and instructions, some of the Israelites faced the dilemma of ceremonial uncleanness at the time of the second annual Passover celebration (their first *commemorative* Passover celebration). Consequently, as the Israelites made preparations for their second Passover, God added even more directives to be followed (Numbers 9:1–14):

11) Everyone had to be ceremonially clean to participate in the Passover.
12) For those who were legitimately unable to participate in the first month of celebration because they were unclean or away on a journey, God showed forbearance and compassion by sanctioning a repetition of the feast on the fourteenth day of the second month.
13) Not observing the feast would result in an individual being cut off from the people.

These additional instructions helped to make a direct connection between observing the Passover celebration and keeping the Mosaic Law. Only those Israelites who were ceremonially clean could participate in the Passover acceptably. While the initial instructions gave details regarding the sacrifice and emphasized their citizenship in physical Israel (as descendants of Abraham through Jacob), these new instructions focused on faithfulness to the new rules of everyday living that God had now given them at Sinai. These additional commands made the Passover commemoration much more vital in the lives of the

Israelites since they were forced to examine themselves to see if they were worthy of participating—that is, that they were ceremonially clean.

Added to these technical instructions was a severe punishment for those who did not celebrate the Passover as prescribed by the Law:

> That person must be cut off from his people because he did not present the LORD's offering at the appointed time. (Numbers 9:13)

While a few commentators take this to be a reference to execution or as a threat of death by God's hand, it most likely refers to exclusion from Israel and its covenant promises. This stipulation demonstrates how serious God was about properly remembering the salvation that he had powerfully accomplished through the Passover. It also confirms the memorial nature of the celebration since, unlike the first Passover, there was no angel of death to be feared or imminent exodus from slavery to be missed by an individual who did not follow God's directives. With these additional instructions, God showed that he fully expected the people that he had saved from slavery in Egypt to demonstrate their devotion and gratitude through a lifetime of faithfulness—not just through one initial act of obedience.

The Third Passover Celebration

When the Israelites finally reached the borders of the promised land, God instructed them to send twelve men into the territory to spy out the land. The majority of the spies brought back faithless and negative reports that caused the people to vehemently complain before the Lord. God was so displeased with their response that he condemned the people of Israel to forty years of wandering in the wilderness—one year for each day the spies had been in the promised land. While the Israelites wandered in the desert, it is evident that they did not keep the Passover properly (or maybe not at all) since none of the children born in the desert were circumcised. They were therefore ceremonially unclean and ineligible to celebrate the Passover (Joshua 5:5–7). Moreover, there was no bread available to use in the Passover meal, for when the Israelites wandered in the desert, they "ate no bread and drank no wine" (Deuteronomy 29:6).

God used the forty years of wandering in the desert as a means of cutting off from the people all who were unwilling to live by faith and believe his promises. Although God had worked so mightily in rescuing his people out of Egypt, he is not sentimental and would not compromise his expectations for faithfulness and obedience. Therefore, as Paul wrote, "God was not pleased with most of them; their bodies were scattered over the desert" (1 Corinthians 10:5). Paul went on to explain that this experience of the Israelites was recorded for our benefit, that we might learn from their example: "So if you think you are standing firm, be careful that you don't fall!" (1 Corinthians 10:12).

As the next generation of Israelites was about to enter the promised land and celebrate the Passover for the third recorded time in history, God made yet further amendments to the regulations concerning its observance (Deuteronomy 16:1–8):

14) The Passover was not to be celebrated in all the towns and cities, but in the one place (city) where God would choose to establish his name.

15) Although the Passover was still to be celebrated by household, all the meat was to be roasted and eaten together in one place. The following morning, all the people could return to their tents.

Interestingly, the first of these amendments annulled the original regulation that the Passover lamb was to be slain at home. Further, the blood was now sprinkled on the altar instead of the lintel and doorposts.

As a clear sign from God that the time of wandering was over, the Israelites began to eat produce from the land. On the second day of the Feast of Unleavened Bread, the manna stopped falling from heaven for the first time in forty years

(Joshua 5:10–12). Thus, the Israelites celebrated this third recorded Passover within the borders of the promised land. These final amendments are the last instructions that we find in the Law of Moses concerning the Passover. They served to reinforce the unity of Israel as one family and its identity as one nation before God.

Other Instances of Celebrating the Passover

Considering the great period of history spanned by the Old Testament, it is remarkable that so few instances of the actual celebration of the Passover are recorded. For the most part, it must simply be assumed that the people of Israel did as they had been commanded. Unfortunately, there were very definite moments in their history when they wandered far from God and his Law, even to the point of not keeping his commandments, feasts and Sabbaths. Examples of two such times are the periods predating the reigns of Hezekiah (2 Chronicles 30:1–27) and Josiah (2 Kings 23:21–23, 2 Chronicles 35:1–19). The fact that the Passover was reinstituted after years of sin and neglect is clear from the details given of these spiritual revivals. Of particular note is the predicament of Hezekiah. When it became clear that many of the Israelites were ceremonially unclean, exceptional restorative measures were taken. The Levites were required to slaughter many of the Passover lambs instead of the heads of households. Also, Hezekiah prayed for God's mercy on all the unclean participants, and God responded positively by healing the people from their impurity.

This situation gives us some insight into God's heart. It was clearly more important to God that the Israelites were showing a renewed desire to seek him than that they simply fulfill the prerequisites found in the Law. God was more inclined to show mercy than to enforce the law's requirements with these penitent Israelites. The zeal of Josiah stands out as well. His first Passover celebration is recorded as being more splendid than that of any king of Israel before him.

The last revival of the Passover celebration in the Old Testament took place after the exiles returned from Babylonian captivity and finished rebuilding the temple (Ezra 6:19–21). After the temple was dedicated, the first feast to be celebrated in Jerusalem was the Passover. All the priests and Levites purified themselves to be ceremonially clean. Without any clear explanation, the Bible records that only the Levites slaughtered the Passover lamb for all of the exiles and the priests. This particular celebration was also special since it united the returned exiles with some of the descendants of the Israelites who had not been taken into captivity. Those who joined in were willing to separate themselves from the unclean practices of their Gentile neighbors in order to seek the Lord. This is the last inspired record we have of the Passover celebration until hundreds of years later when Jesus went up to the temple in Jerusalem with his family to celebrate the Passover feast.

The Foundational Nature of the Passover

The Passover celebration was a very significant event in the Jewish calendar. Its preparation not only marked the first month of the Jewish year, but its inauguration also marked the beginning of Israel's relationship with God as a redeemed nation. In the context of the Mosaic Law with its program of feasts, ceremonial washings and animal sacrifices, the Passover and the Feast of Unleavened Bread were unique for another reason: they were instituted *before* the giving of the Law of Moses and the establishment of the Levitical priesthood. This distinction is important; it means that the proper celebration of the Passover required each individual household—not just those in the priesthood—to take responsibility for their own family's devotion and obedience to God.

God warned the Israelites through Moses about the death of the firstborn. He also promised them protection, contingent upon their faithfulness in keeping all the ordinances of the Passover. Through their voluntary obedience to the conditions of this celebration, God demonstrated the kind of heart he was seeking in the people he was calling out of bondage:

> And now, O Israel, what does the LORD your God ask of you but to fear the LORD your God, to walk in all his ways, to love him, to serve the LORD your God with all your heart and with all your soul, and to observe the LORD's commands and decrees that I am giving you today for your own good? (Deuteronomy 10:12–13)

This mandatory offering was the beginning of a system of sacrifice and worship through which God taught the Israelites the principle of redemption: the process of making payment to purchase something or to set free from obligation. God could have simply wiped out the Egyptians with a word and let the Israelites walk freely out of Egypt. He chose instead to demonstrate the price of their salvation through the death of the firstborn of Egypt and the blood of their sacrificial lambs. Since it had been decreed that all firstborn males of both man and beast (even those belonging to the Israelites) should die, God bought the lives of the firstborn of Israel through the blood of the Passover lambs.

Salvation from bondage in Egypt was a free gift from God and was not forced upon anyone. God nonetheless set forth conditions for the Israelites that had to be fulfilled so that the people could respond in faith to his offer. There was nothing inherent in the blood of a lamb or in its ritual sacrifice that caused the angel of death to pass over the homes of the Israelites. The Passover lamb was able to redeem their firstborn from death simply because God had ordained the sacrifice to be an acceptable substitute as well as an expression of faith in his word. God purposefully set up all the regulations of the Passover sacrifice for their instructional and faith-demonstrating value. The ordinances of the Law took this principle even further by providing sacrifice for the removal of guilt and sin—both of the nation and of the individual. There is an implied parallel between the Passover sacrifice and the Mosaic sacrificial system: sin means bondage and death, and righteousness brings freedom and life. In Leviticus 17:11 this idea is more clearly explained:

> For the life of a creature is in the blood, and I have given it to you to make atonement for yourselves on the altar; it is the blood that makes atonement for one's life.

The penalty for sin has been death since the very beginning. Therefore it is only through the sacrifice of blood—the giving of a life—that atonement for sin can be made.[4]

Not only did the Passover mark the beginning of a new system of redemption for God's people based on animal sacrifice, but the redemption of the firstborn of Israel also gave rise to the setting apart of the Levites for a special role of service. Since the lives of all the firstborn of Israel belonged to God after the angel of death passed over them, God redeemed the debt by accepting the whole tribe of Levi as payment in their place (Numbers 3:5–13, 8:5–26). The Levites were set apart from the other Israelites to perform duties for Aaron's descendants (the priests) and for the whole community at the Tent of Meeting by serving at the tabernacle. The Levites were supported through portions of the sacrifices and through the tithe and were not given a geographical inheritance with the other tribes of Israel, though they did receive forty-eight cities throughout the land. And while the Levites served the whole community of Israel in this way, there was never any instruction for the household leaders to stop preparing their annual Passover sacrifices or for the priests or Levites to officially take over this responsibility.

Summary

The Passover celebration was hugely significant for the people of Israel from the moment of its inception. The laws that governed the Passover were revised and amended as the Israelites went through various stages of their journey to the promised land. This happened not only because the living conditions of the Israelites changed as they journeyed, but also because of the further revelation of God's commands and regulations for everyday living.

The first set of regulations mainly focused on the practical aspects surrounding the observance, including selection, preparation and consumption of the sacrifice. Some of the initial regulations also applied specifically to the immediate working out of their salvation, such as marking their doorposts and lintels with blood for the angel of death to see and thereby pass over, as well as eating with haste, being dressed and ready to flee. Although the continued observance of these regulations caused the next generation to ask good questions and thus reinforced the commemorative nature of the Passover, it would seem that they were disregarded once the Israelites were together in one place in the promised land.

The Passover celebration began as a family gathering in which the head of each household was wholly responsible for preparing the sacrifice and teaching his family the method and the meaning of the event. By the time the Israelites entered the promised land, the Passover was still to be observed by household, but the people were required to come together in one place for the celebration, reinforcing their unity as a nation before God. Initially, there was no punishment legislated for those who refused to correctly observe the Passover, since the consequence was inherently disastrous—the death of the first-born of both man and livestock.

In the following years, when the Passover became strictly commemorative, regulations were added to reinforce the exclusiveness of God's chosen people. Circumcision and ceremonial cleanness became prerequisites to participation in the Passover. The requirement that all males be circumcised served as a sign of their relationship to the covenant that God had made with Abraham. It also demonstrated that, through circumcision, a non-Israelite could actually be counted as an Israelite before God.

With the receiving of the Law, the Israelites were educated as to the meaning of ceremonial cleanness. God then added new regulations to make sure that those who participated in the Passover were in good standing according to the Law. It was also decreed that those who disregarded the Passover and failed to keep the regulations were to be cut off from the people. That the Passover was apparently not celebrated by the Israelites during the forty years in the desert underscores the fact that God cut off that generation from their inheritance in the promised land.

Considering the significance of the Passover celebration to the nation of Israel, it is not surprising that in times of renewal and rededication, the Passover was often the first feast reinstituted. In such times of spiritual revival, God demonstrated his love for those seeking to do his will and was mercifully lenient with regard to the requirements for ceremonial cleanness. If the people of God would realign their hearts to the meaning of the Passover, then keeping the Law would naturally follow.

The Israelites were tempted time and again to think they were special because they had knowledge of the Law and possessed the promised land. God intended for the annual Passover celebration to be a powerful reminder that the uniqueness of the Israelites was due to the covenant he had made with Abraham and to the great salvation he had worked by bringing them up out of Egypt. After God brought the Israelites through the Red Sea, he directed Moses to tell the Israelites:

> "You yourselves have seen what I did to Egypt, and how I carried you on eagles' wings and brought you to myself. Now if you obey me fully and keep my covenant, then out of all nations you will be my treasured possession. Although the whole earth is mine, you will be for me a kingdom of priests and a holy nation." (Exodus 19:3–6)

The celebration of the Passover was a powerful demonstration of the meaning of this scripture. The whole nation of Israel participated as they sacrificed their own Passover lambs by household, and this reminded them that they were called out of bondage by God to be a people separate from the other nations. The exodus from Egypt was much more than just the release of an enslaved people. It was the product of God's covenant with Abraham and an invitation for a whole nation to become the people of God through personal faithfulness to the conditions of his covenant with them.

Jesus clearly chose the Passover as the setting for establishing the Lord's Supper. And while the richness of this setting should not be ignored, we must be careful not to read more into the association than is warranted by Scripture; as Paul admonished the Corinthians, "Do not go beyond that which is written" (1 Corinthians 4:6). For instance, there is no reason to assume that any of the laws regulating the observance of Passover were ever meant to be transferred to the taking of the Lord's Supper. Such strict regulations and possible penalties for disobedience were not the focus of Christ, whose teaching was centered on the attitudes of the heart. On the other hand, the better we understand all aspects of this central Jewish feast, the more fully we will appreciate the meaning-soaked environment in which Jesus' own memorial meal came into being.

Notes

1. In Genesis 22, Abraham and his son Isaac set out to offer a burnt offering to God on one of the mountains. Isaac expected that there would be a singular lamb offered, but that may have been simply because of some comment his father had already made. As they journeyed to the place of sacrifice, Isaac wanted to know where the lamb was, since they did not have one in their possession. Abraham assured his son that God would provide one—and he did. Other recorded instances of burnt offerings and sacrifices that predated the Passover are as follows:

- Cain offered some of the fruits of the soil as an offering, but Abel offered God the fat portions of some of the firstborn of his flock. God looked with favor on Abel's offering but did not look with favor on Cain's (Genesis 4:4–5).
- Noah offered some of all the clean animals after the ark had settled on dry land (Genesis 8:20).
- Abraham offered a heifer, a goat and a ram (all three-year-olds), and a pigeon and a dove (Genesis 15:9–21). This was done as part of a ceremony to ratify his covenant with God.
- Jacob offered an unspecified sacrifice with Laban, and his relatives shared in the meal together with him (Genesis 31:54–55).
- Jacob offered unspecified sacrifices on his way down to Egypt (Genesis 45:26–46:1).

2. The fact that the lamb was to be totally consumed by sunrise may explain the direction to roast the meat—raw meat could have possibly dripped blood and boiled meat would have produced a broth.

3. I make this suggestion because of personal experience gained while serving as a missionary in Papua New Guinea. I was told of natives who stole away pieces of the communion bread from the church services to place inside amulets and to use secretly in other pagan rituals.

4. This Hebrew word for *atonement* literally means "covering" and has an interesting parallel with the first recorded shedding of blood in the Bible. Although Adam and Eve had made clothing for themselves after they sinned and realized that they were naked, they still hid themselves from God when he came to visit with them in the garden. Their own attempt at covering their nakedness seemed to work between themselves, but it was not effective in removing their shame and guilt before God. After God confronted them about their sin and pronounced his judgments upon them, we read in Genesis 3:21: "The Lord God made garments of skin for Adam and his wife and clothed them." Once their covering was "God-approved," they were able to continue in their relationship with God in good conscience. Even from the beginning, the cost of man's atonement (covering) was the taking of life—the shedding of blood.

2

The Passover Celebration
First Century Jewish Tradition

I f we are to fully understand the origins of the Lord's Supper, we must turn our attention to the way that the Passover was celebrated in the time of Jesus. The society and politics of Judea underwent many turbulent changes from the time of the remnant's return in the fifth century BC until the first century AD. The exile and dispersion of many Jews, together with the destruction and rebuilding of the temple, had a great impact on their forms of worship and religious instruction. The struggle of the Jewish people for self-rule and self-determination influenced their religious beliefs as well.

Judaism in the first century was known for its religious division, a situation that had been evolving for at least two centuries. Considering the conditions that allowed for these sectarian developments, it is not surprising that the customs surrounding the celebration of Passover also experienced some modification and revision.

By about AD 217 a Jewish commentary called the Mishnah was put into writing.[1] Reflecting the oral "traditions of the elders" (Matthew 15:2), it addressed concrete questions of how the Old Testament Law was to be observed and practiced. The Mishnah is divided into topical sections, and its format is comprised of statements of interpretation of the Law, followed by the commentary of certain rabbis or schools of rabbis. The customs outlined in this document shed some interesting light on the traditions of the Jews during the first century with regard to the Passover, as well as on details preserved in the Gospels about Passover celebrations during the lifetime of Jesus.

Significantly, the Mishnah has never come under the influence of the church or of Jews converted to Christianity, a development that might have led critics to discredit its testimony. For this reason, its verification of specific details in the Gospel accounts carries great credibility.

The Passover (*Pesachim*)

As noted in chapter 1, the observance of Passover was modified after the Israelites received the Law and the priesthood, and again when they finally came to possess the promised land. The Mishnah reaffirms these changes in its discussion of the Passover:

> What is the difference between the Passover of Egypt and the Passover of the succeeding generations? As to the Passover of Egypt—
>
>   (1) [the lamb's] designation took place on the tenth of Nisan;
>
>   (2) it required sprinkling of the blood of the lamb with a branch of hyssop on the lintel of the door and on the two doorposts; and
>
>   (3) it was eaten in haste in a single night.
>
> But the Passover observed by the succeeding generations applies [to leaven] for all seven days [and not only for one night]. (Pesachim 9:5)

Blood was no longer painted on the lintel and doorposts, and being dressed ready to flee was no longer considered a requirement. In addition, it appears that in time the Passover celebration and the subsequent seven days of the Feast of Unleavened Bread had merged in people's minds to become one festival.

The Mishnah also describes the formula for the *household* celebration of the Passover. These details are of immense interest to us since they supply an explanation for otherwise random details given in the Gospels that would have been understood by first century readers. The precise application of these rules to Jesus and his disciples is slightly clouded by the fact that these directives were intended for a physical family and not necessarily for a rabbi and his followers. The fact that Jesus gathered his disciples as his family on this particular Passover, however, makes a strong statement about his heart toward his disciples. As we review the following instructions, notice the atmosphere created by this scripted custom, as well as the number of small details that are also evident in the Gospel accounts of the evening of Jesus' betrayal.

> On the eve of Passover from just before the afternoon's daily whole offering, a person should not eat, until it gets dark. And even the poorest Israelite should not eat until he reclines at his table.[2] And they should provide him with no fewer than four cups of wine...
>
> When they have mixed the first cup of wine—the House of Shammai say, "He says a blessing over the day, and afterward he says a blessing over the wine." The House of Hillel say, "He says a blessing over the wine, and afterward he says a blessing over the day."
>
> [When] they bring him [the food], he dips the lettuce [in vinegar] before he comes to the breaking of the bread. They brought him unleavened bread, lettuce and haroset[3] and two dishes...and in the time of the Temple they would bring before him the carcass of the Passover offering.
>
> They mixed for him a second cup of wine. And here the son asks his father [questions]. But if the son has not got the intelligence to do so, the father teaches him [to ask by pointing out]:
>
>> "How different is this night from all other nights! For on all other nights we eat leavened or unleavened bread. But this night all of the bread is unleavened. For on all other nights we eat diverse vegetables, but on this night, only bitter herbs. For on all other nights we eat meat which is roasted, stewed or boiled. But this night all of the meat is roasted. For on all other nights we dip our food one time, but on this night two times."
>
> In accord with the intelligence of the son, the father instructs him. He begins [answering the questions] with disgrace and concludes with glory, and explains [the Scriptures from], "A wandering Aramean was my father..."[4] until he completes the entire section.
>
> Rabban Gamaliel did state, "Whoever has not referred to these three matters connected to the Passover has not fulfilled his obligation, and these are they: Passover, unleavened bread, and bitter herbs.

"Passover—because the Omnipresent passed over the houses of our forefathers in Egypt.

"Unleavened bread—because our forefathers were redeemed in Egypt.

"Bitter herbs—because the Egyptians embittered the lives of our forefathers in Egypt."

In every generation a person is duty-bound to regard himself as if he personally has gone forth from Egypt, since it is said, "And you shall tell your son in that day saying, 'It is because of that which the Lord did for me when I came forth out of Egypt.'[5] Therefore we are duty-bound to thank, praise, glorify, honor, exalt, extol, and bless him who did for our forefathers and for us all these miracles. He brought us forth from slavery to freedom, anguish to joy, mourning to festival, darkness to great light, subjugation to redemption, so we should say before him, Hallelujah."

...And he concludes with [a formula of] Redemption. Rabbi Tarfon says, "...who redeemed us and redeemed our forefathers from Egypt." And he did not say a concluding benediction. Rabbi Aqiba says, "...So, Lord, our God, and God of our fathers, bring us in peace to other appointed times and festivals, rejoicing in the rebuilding of your city and joyful in your Temple worship, where may we eat of the animal sacrifices and Passover offerings," etc., up to, "Blessed are you, Lord, who has redeemed Israel."

They mixed the third cup for him. He says a blessing for his food. [And at] the fourth, he completes the Hallel and says after it the grace of song....[6]

The Passover offering after midnight [at which point it may no longer be eaten] imparts uncleanness to hands. That which is made refuse and remnant impart uncleanness to the hands.... (Pesachim 10:1–9)

The celebration of the Passover by household was ordained by God and, when done as intended, provided an incredibly meaningful program for teaching the subsequent generations about the details of Israel's deliverance from Egypt. Although the Mishnah demonstrates that there were some small disagreements among the traditions of how the Passover was to be celebrated, the overall tone and events of the evening were well defined and thought out. Jesus must have been well supplied with thoughts and commentary concerning the meal that was about to take place. This description of the Passover is of great value as we seek to imagine the circumstances surrounding the introduction of the Lord's Supper on the evening of Christ's betrayal.

Blessings and Prayers (*Berakhot*)

Another insight from the Mishnah comes from its discussion of agricultural blessings and prayers. Here we find use of the phrase "fruit of the vine," an expression not found in the Old Testament.

> What blessing does one recite over produce? Over fruit of a tree he says, "[Blessed are you, O Lord, our God, King of the Universe,] Creator of the fruit of the tree," except for wine. For over wine he says, "Creator of the fruit of the vine." (Berakhot 6:1)

Flavius Josephus, the first century Jewish historian, also attests to this figure of speech. As he recounts the story of how the patriarch Joseph interpreted the royal cupbearer's dream in prison, he refers to wine as "the fruit of the vine."[7]

Summary

In the context of the Roman occupation, the Passover celebration added fuel to the nationalistic pride and zeal of the Jewish people. The act of remembering God's deliverance from the bondage of Egypt could not help but evoke a longing for freedom from Roman rule. Redemption was still the good news for which the Jewish people were living and waiting—centuries after God had accomplished his feat in Egypt.

By the time of the New Testament period, the Passover celebration had adopted some additional regulations and customs, as was the case with many other aspects of practical Judaism. One of the most reliable sources of information concerning these developments is the Mishnah, a collection of rabbinical teachings on various topics related to the Law of Moses that dates back in written form to the early third century AD. It is quite clear, even to the casual reader of the New Testament, that the Gospels confirm the existence of a number of these additional customs.

Of particular note to our study of the Lord's Supper are the reclining at the table and the inclusion of wine at the Passover celebration. The stipulation of being dressed ready to flee had been replaced by a much more relaxed posture. And by the first century AD, the drinking of wine (mixed with water) had become an integral part of the ceremony, with at least four shared cups punctuating the evening's activities. According to the Mishnah, these four cups were also connected to different benedictions, blessings, scripture readings and instructions, although the Old Testament never made mention of such an elaborate program. The fact that the wine was referred to as the "fruit of the vine" also reflects the influence of the customs of this period.

A review of these first century customs gives the student of the New Testament an opportunity to appreciate more fully what was going through the minds of Christ's disciples as they gathered to celebrate the Passover. Their expectations as to what was supposed to take place were well-established, and any deviation from the usual celebration would have been noticeable and significant.

Notes

1. For an accessible English translation, see Jacob Neusner, *The Mishnah: A New Translation*, (New Haven & London: Yale University Press, 1988).

2. Reclining at the table was typical for a first century Palestinian festive dinner, and for the Jews it even may have been a gesture of Israel's liberation from bondage (*Jerome Biblical Commentary,* Joseph A. Fitzmyer, S.J., editor of NT commentary articles, Volume II, Logos Online Version, 1990).

3. Haroset is a relish made of fruits and spices with vinegar or wine, used to sweeten the bitter herb at the Passover meal.

4. Deuteronomy 26:5ff

5. Exodus 13:8ff

6. The "Hallel" is a portion of the liturgy, consisting of Psalms 113–118, recited on festivals and new moons.

7. *The Works of Josephus,* (Oak Harbor, Wash.: Logos Research Systems, Inc., 1997). The Jews may have preferred this figure to de-emphasize the intoxicating nature of wine in contrast to pagan festivals in which drunkenness was ritualistic. It is noteworthy that Jesus chose this figure, and not a possible Old Testament figure, "blood of the grape," as found in Genesis 49:11 and Deuteronomy 32:14.

3

The Evening Jesus Was Betrayed

A s the earthly ministry of Jesus neared its climax and culmination, he tried to get his closest disciples to understand the amazing events that were about to be fulfilled. Leading his disciples toward Jerusalem, Jesus took the Twelve aside and told them yet again of his impending betrayal, suffering, condemnation, death and resurrection (Matthew 20:17–19, Mark 10:32–24, Luke 18:31–34). Although the plan was clear in Jesus' mind and the time of fulfillment plainly at hand, not one of his disciples understood the significance of the events that were about to take place. The interactions of the Son of God with his disciples give us a context for understanding the teaching of Jesus and his incredible patience and love in dealing with each one of us. The disciples did not yet understand that the Messiah and the "Suffering Servant" of Isaiah 53 were one and the same person, and the greatest sacrifice in all of history was about to take place.

The Gospels provide us with a detailed account of what took place on the evening Jesus was betrayed. While Matthew and Mark provide identical accounts, Luke and John make distinctive contributions to the detail of the narrative. By compiling the four passages (Matthew 26:17–56, Mark 14:12–50, Luke 22:7–53 and John 13:2–18:12) into a single account, we can obtain a more complete picture of what the disciples experienced that evening.[1] While we cannot be absolutely certain of the exact chronology of events, the reconstruction that follows maintains the order as given in each Gospel rather than assuming that similar incidents were identical events that were recorded out of sequence.[2]

For ease of reference, the compiled chronology below is divided into sections with the source texts given in each heading. Although these verses may be very familiar to you, take time to read through this inspiring account. It represents our primary source of information regarding the establishment of the Lord's Supper. Each of us needs to put ourselves in the place of the disciples and then of Jesus. This will help us to acknowledge the weakness or strength of our conclusions—and to be impressed by Christ's love and obedience to the Father.

John 13:1

It was just before the Passover Feast. Jesus knew that the time had come for him to leave this world and go to the Father. Having loved his own who were in the world, he now showed them the full extent of his love.

Matthew 26:17–19, Mark 14:12–16, Luke 22:7–13

On the first day of the Feast of Unleavened Bread, when it was customary to sacrifice the Passover lamb, Jesus' disciples asked him, "Where do you want us to go and make preparations for you to eat the Passover?"

Jesus sent Peter and John, saying, "Go into the city, and a man carrying a jar of water will meet you. Follow him. Say to the owner of the house he enters, 'The Teacher asks: Where is my guest room, where I may eat the Passover with my disciples?' He will show you a large upper room, furnished and ready. Make preparations for us there." The disciples left, went into the city and found things just as Jesus had told them. So the disciples did as Jesus had directed them and prepared the Passover.

Matthew 26:20, Mark 14:18, Luke 22:14

When evening came, Jesus arrived with the Twelve. Jesus and his apostles reclined at the table.

Luke 22:15–18

And he said to them, "I have eagerly desired to eat this Passover with you before I suffer. For I tell you, I will not eat it again until it finds fulfillment in the kingdom of God." After taking the cup, he gave thanks and said, "Take this and divide it among you. For I tell you I will not drink again of the fruit of the vine until the kingdom of God comes."

John 13:2

The evening meal was being served, and the devil had already prompted Judas Iscariot, son of Simon, to betray Jesus.

Matthew 26:21–25, Mark 14:18–21

While they were reclining at the table eating, he said, "I tell you the truth, one of you will betray me—one who is eating with me." They were very sad and began to say to him one after the other, "Surely not I, Lord?"

"It is one of the Twelve," Jesus replied. "The one who has dipped his hand into the bowl with me will betray me. The Son of Man will go just as it is written about him. But woe to that man who betrays the Son of Man! It would be better for him if he had not been born."

Then Judas, the one who would betray him, said, "Surely not I, Rabbi?"

Jesus answered, "Yes, it is you."

Matthew 26:26–29, Mark 14:22–25, Luke 22:19–20

And while they were eating, Jesus took bread, gave thanks and broke it, and gave it to his disciples, saying, "Take it and eat; this is my body given for you; do this in remembrance of me."

Then, in the same way after the supper he took the cup, gave thanks and offered it to them, saying, "Drink from it, all of you," and they all drank from it.[3] "This is my blood of the new covenant, which is poured out for many for the forgiveness of sins," he said to them. "I tell you the truth, I will not drink of the fruit of the vine again until that day when I drink it anew in my Father's kingdom.

Luke 22:21–24

"But the hand of him who is going to betray me is with mine on the table. The Son of Man will go as it has been decreed, but woe to that man who betrays him." They began to question among themselves which of them it might be who would do this. Also a dispute arose among them as to which of them was considered to be greatest.

John 13:3–11

Jesus knew that the Father had put all things under his power, and that he had come from God and was returning to God; so he got up from the meal, took off his outer clothing, and wrapped a towel around his waist. After that, he poured water into a basin and began to wash his disciples' feet, drying them with the towel that was wrapped around him.

He came to Simon Peter, who said to him, "Lord, are you going to wash my feet?"

Jesus replied, "You do not realize now what I am doing, but later you will understand."

"No," said Peter, "you shall never wash my feet."

Jesus answered, "Unless I wash you, you have no part with me."

"Then, Lord," Simon Peter replied, "not just my feet but my hands and my head as well!"

Jesus answered, "A person who has had a bath needs only to wash his feet; his whole body is clean. And you are clean, though not every one of you." For he knew who was going to betray him, and that was why he said not every one was clean.

Luke 22:25–27, John 13:12–17

When he had finished washing their feet, he put on his clothes and returned to his place. "Do you understand what I have done for you?" he asked them.

"You call me 'Teacher' and 'Lord,' and rightly so, for that is what I am. Now that I, your Lord and Teacher, have washed your feet, you also should wash one another's feet. I have set you an example that you should do as I have done for you. I tell you the truth, no servant is greater than his master, nor is a messenger greater than the one who sent him."

Jesus said to them, "The kings of the Gentiles lord it over them; and those who exercise authority over them call themselves Benefactors. But you are not to be like that. Instead, the greatest among you should be like the youngest, and the one who rules like the one who serves. For who is greater, the one who is at the table or the one who serves? Is it not the one who is at the table? But I am among you as one who serves.

"Now that you know these things, you will be blessed if you do them."

John 13:18–36

"I am not referring to all of you; I know those I have chosen. But this is to fulfill the scripture: 'He who shares my bread has lifted up his heel against me.'

"I am telling you now before it happens, so that when it does happen you will believe that I am he. I tell you the truth, whoever accepts anyone I send accepts me; and whoever accepts me accepts the one who sent me."

After he had said this, Jesus was troubled in spirit and testified, "I tell you the truth, one of you is going to betray me."

His disciples stared at one another, at a loss to know which of them he meant. One of them, the disciple whom Jesus loved, was reclining next to him. Simon Peter motioned to this disciple and said, "Ask him which one he means."

Leaning back against Jesus, he asked him, "Lord, who is it?"

Jesus answered, "It is the one to whom I will give this piece of bread when I have dipped it in the dish." Then, dipping the piece of bread, he gave it to Judas Iscariot, son of Simon. As soon as Judas took the bread, Satan entered into him.

"What you are about to do, do quickly," Jesus told him, but no one at the meal understood why Jesus said this to him. Since Judas had charge of the money, some thought Jesus was telling him to buy what was need- ed for the Feast, or to give something to the poor. As soon as Judas had taken the bread, he went out. And it was night.

When he was gone, Jesus said, "Now is the Son of Man glorified and God is glorified in him. If God is glorified in him, God will glorify the Son in himself, and will glorify him at once.

"My children, I will be with you only a little longer. You will look for me, and just as I told the Jews, so I tell you now: Where I am going, you can- not come.

"A new command I give you: Love one another. As I have loved you, so you must love one another. By this all men will know that you are my disciples, if you love one another."

Simon Peter asked him, "Lord, where are you going?"

Jesus replied, "Where I am going, you cannot follow now, but you will follow later."

Luke 22:28–30

"You are those who have stood by me in my trials. And I confer on you a kingdom, just as my Father conferred one on me, so that you may eat and drink at my table in my kingdom and sit on thrones, judging the twelve tribes of Israel."

Luke 22:31–34, John 13:37–38

"Simon, Simon, Satan has asked to sift you as wheat. But I have prayed for you, Simon, that your faith may not fail. And when you have turned back, strengthen your brothers."

But he replied, "Lord, I am ready to go with you to prison and to death." Peter asked, "Lord, why can't I follow you now? I will lay down my life for you."

Then Jesus answered, "Will you really lay down your life for me? I tell you the truth, Peter, before the rooster crows today, you will deny three times that you know me!"

John 14:1–31

"Do not let your hearts be troubled. Trust in God; trust also in me. In my Father's house are many rooms; if it were not so, I would have told you. I am going there to prepare a place for you. And if I go and prepare a place for you, I will come back and take you to be with me that you also may be where I am. You know the way to the place where I am going."

Thomas said to him, "Lord, we don't know where you are going, so how can we know the way?"

Jesus answered, "I am the way and the truth and the life. No one comes to the Father except through me. If you really knew me, you would know my Father as well. From now on, you do know him and have seen him."

Philip said, "Lord, show us the Father and that will be enough for us."

Jesus answered: "Don't you know me, Philip, even after I have been among you such a long time? Anyone who has seen me has seen the Father. How can you say, 'Show us the Father'? Don't you believe that I am in the Father, and that the Father is in me? The words I say to you are not just my own. Rather, it is the Father, living in me, who is doing his work. Believe me when I say that I am in the Father and the Father is in me; or at least believe on the evidence of the miracles themselves. I tell you the truth, anyone who has faith in me will do what I have been doing. He will do even greater things than these, because I am going to the Father. And I will do whatever you ask in my name, so that the Son may bring glory to the Father. You may ask me for anything in my name, and I will do it.

"If you love me, you will obey what I command. And I will ask the Father, and he will give you another Counselor to be with you forever— the Spirit of truth. The world cannot accept him, because it neither sees him nor knows him. But you know him, for he lives with you and will be in you. I will not leave you as orphans; I will come to you. Before long, the world will not see me anymore, but you will see me. Because I live, you also will live. On that day you will realize that I am in my Father, and you are in me, and I am in you. Whoever has my commands and obeys them, he is the one who loves me. He who loves me will be loved by my Father, and I too will love him and show myself to him."

Then Judas (not Judas Iscariot) said, "But, Lord, why do you intend to show yourself to us and not to the world?"

Jesus replied, "If anyone loves me, he will obey my teaching. My Father will love him, and we will come to him and make our home with him. He who does not love me will not obey my teaching. These words you hear are not my own; they belong to the Father who sent me.

"All this I have spoken while still with you. But the Counselor, the Holy Spirit, whom the Father will send in my name, will teach you all things and will remind you of everything I have said to you. Peace I leave with you; my peace I give you. I do not give to you as the world gives. Do not let your hearts be troubled and do not be afraid.

"You heard me say, 'I am going away and I am coming back to you.' If you loved me, you would be glad that I am going to the Father, for the Father is greater than I. I have told you now before it happens, so that when it does happen you will believe. I will not speak with you much longer, for the prince of this world is coming. He has no hold on me, but the world must learn that I love the Father and that I do exactly what my Father has commanded me."

Luke 22:35–38

Then Jesus asked them, "When I sent you without purse, bag or sandals, did you lack anything?"

"Nothing," they answered.

He said to them, "But now if you have a purse, take it, and also a bag; and if you don't have a sword, sell your cloak and buy one. It is written: 'And he was numbered with the transgressors'; and I tell you that this must be fulfilled in me. Yes, what is written about me is reaching its fulfillment."

The disciples said, "See, Lord, here are two swords."

"That is enough," he replied.

Matthew 26:30, Mark 14:26, Luke 22:39, John 14:31

"Come now; let us leave."

When they had sung a hymn, Jesus went out as usual to the Mount of Olives, and his disciples followed him.

John 15:1–16:31

"I am the true vine, and my Father is the gardener. He cuts off every branch in me that bears no fruit, while every branch that does bear fruit he prunes so that it will be even more fruitful. You are already clean because of the word I have spoken to you. Remain in me, and I will remain in you. No branch can bear fruit by itself; it must remain in the vine. Neither can you bear fruit unless you remain in me.

"I am the vine; you are the branches. If a man remains in me and I in him, he will bear much fruit; apart from me you can do nothing. If anyone does not remain in me, he is like a branch that is thrown away and withers; such branches are picked up, thrown into the fire and burned. If you remain in me and my words remain in you, ask whatever you wish, and it will be given you. This is to my Father's glory, that you bear much fruit, showing yourselves to be my disciples.

"As the Father has loved me, so have I loved you. Now remain in my love. If you obey my commands, you will remain in my love, just as I have obeyed my Father's commands and remain in his love. I have told you this so that my joy may be in you and that your joy may be complete. My command is this: Love each other as I have loved you. Greater love has no one than this, that he lay down his life for his friends. You are my friends if you do what I command. I no longer call you servants, because a servant does not know his master's business. Instead, I have called you friends, for everything that I learned from my Father I have made known to you. You did not choose me, but I chose you and appointed you to go and bear fruit—fruit that will last. Then the Father will give you whatever you ask in my name. This is my command: Love each other.

"If the world hates you, keep in mind that it hated me first. If you belonged to the world, it would love you as its own. As it is, you do not belong to the world, but I have chosen you out of the world. That is why the world hates you. Remember the words I spoke to you: 'No servant is greater than his master.' If they persecuted me, they will persecute you also. If they obeyed my teaching, they will obey yours also. They will treat you this way because of my name, for they do not know the One who sent me. If I had not come and spoken to them, they would not be guilty of sin. Now, however, they have no excuse for their sin. He who hates me hates my Father as well. If I had not done among them what no one else did, they would not be guilty of sin. But now they have seen these miracles, and yet they have hated both me and my Father. But this is to fulfill what is written in their Law: 'They hated me without reason.'

"When the Counselor comes, whom I will send to you from the Father, the Spirit of truth who goes out from the Father, he will testify about me. And you also must testify, for you have been with me from the beginning.

"All this I have told you so that you will not go astray. They will put you out of the synagogue; in fact, a time is coming when anyone who kills you will think he is offering a service to God. They will do such things because they have not known the Father or me. I have told you this, so that when the time comes you will remember that I warned you. I did not tell you this at first because I was with you.

"Now I am going to him who sent me, yet none of you asks me, 'Where are you going?' Because I have said these things, you are filled with grief. But I tell you the truth: It is for your good that I am going away. Unless I go away, the Counselor will not come to you; but if I go, I will send him to you. When he comes, he will convict the world of guilt in regard to sin and right-eousness and judgment: in regard to sin, because men do not believe in me; in regard to righteousness, because I am going to the Father, where you can see me no longer; and in regard to judgment, because the prince of this world now stands condemned.

"I have much more to say to you, more than you can now bear. But when he, the Spirit of truth, comes, he will guide you into all truth. He will not speak on his own; he will speak only what he hears, and he will tell you what is yet to come. He will bring glory to me by taking from what is mine and making it known to you. All that belongs to the Father is mine. That is why I said the Spirit will take from what is mine and make it known to you.

"In a little while you will see me no more, and then after a little while you will see me."

Some of his disciples said to one another, "What does he mean by saying, 'In a little while you will see me no more, and then after a little while you will see me,' and 'Because I am going to the Father'?" They kept asking, "What does he mean by 'a little while'? We don't understand what he is saying."

Jesus saw that they wanted to ask him about this, so he said to them, "Are you asking one another what I meant when I said, 'In a little while you will see me no more, and then after a little while you will see me'? I tell you the truth, you will weep and mourn while the world rejoices. You will grieve, but your grief will turn to joy. A woman giving birth to a child has pain because her time has come; but when her baby is born she forgets the anguish because of her joy that a child is born into the world. So with you: Now is your time of grief, but I will see you again and you will rejoice, and no one will take away your joy. In that day you will no longer ask me anything. I tell you the truth, my Father will give you whatever you ask in my name. Until now you have not asked for anything in my name. Ask and you will receive, and your joy will be complete.

"Though I have been speaking figuratively, a time is coming when I will no longer use this kind of language but will tell you plainly about my Father. In that day you will ask in my name. I am not saying that I will ask the Father on your behalf. No, the Father himself loves you because you have loved me and have believed that I came from God. I came from the Father and entered the world; now I am leaving the world and going back to the Father."

Then Jesus' disciples said, "Now you are speaking clearly and without figures of speech. Now we can see that you know all things and that you do not even need to have anyone ask you questions. This makes us believe that you came from God."

"You believe at last!" Jesus answered.

Matthew 26:31–32, Mark 14:27–28, John 16:32–33

Then Jesus told them, "But a time is coming, and has come, when you will be scattered, each to his own home. You will leave me all alone. Yet I am not alone, for my Father is with me. This very night you will all fall away on account of me, for it is written:

"'I will strike the shepherd,
and the sheep of the flock will be scattered.'

But after I have risen, I will go ahead of you into Galilee.

"I have told you these things, so that in me you may have peace. In this world you will have trouble. But take heart! I have overcome the world."

Matthew 26:33–35, Mark 14:29–31

Peter replied, "Even if all fall away on account of you, I never will."

"I tell you the truth," Jesus answered, "today—yes, tonight—before the rooster crows twice you yourself will disown me three times."

But Peter insisted emphatically, "Even if I have to die with you, I will never disown you." And all the other disciples said the same.

John 17:1–26

After Jesus said this, he looked toward heaven and prayed:

"Father, the time has come. Glorify your Son, that your Son may glorify you. For you granted him authority over all people that he might give eternal life to all those you have given him. Now this is eternal life: that they may know you, the only true God, and Jesus Christ, whom you have sent. I have brought you glory on earth by completing the work you gave me to do. And now, Father, glorify me in your presence with the glory I had with you before the world began.

"I have revealed you to those whom you gave me out of the world. They were yours; you gave them to me and they have obeyed your word. Now they know that everything you have given me comes from you. For I gave them the words you gave me and they accepted them. They knew with certainty that I came from you, and they believed that you sent me. I pray for them. I am not praying for the world, but for those you have given me, for they are yours. All I have is yours, and all you have is mine. And glory has come to me through them. I will remain in the world no longer, but they are still in the world, and I am coming to you. Holy Father, protect them by the power of your name—the name you gave me—so that they may be one as we are one. While I was with them, I protected them and kept them safe by that name you gave me. None has been lost except the one doomed to destruction so that Scripture would be fulfilled.

"I am coming to you now, but I say these things while I am still in the world, so that they may have the full measure of my joy within them. I have given them your word and the world has hated them, for they are not of the world any more than I am of the world. My prayer is not that you take them out of the world but that you protect them from the evil one. They are not of the world, even as I am not of it. Sanctify them by the truth; your word is truth. As you sent me into the world, I have sent them into the world. For them I sanctify myself, that they too may be truly sanctified.

"My prayer is not for them alone. I pray also for those who will believe in me through their message, that all of them may be one, Father, just as you are in me and I am in you. May they also be in us so that the world may believe that you have sent me. I have given them the glory that you gave me, that they may be one as we are one: I in them and you in me. May they be brought to complete unity to let the world know that you sent me and have loved them even as you have loved me.

"Father, I want those you have given me to be with me where I am, and to see my glory, the glory you have given me because you loved me before the creation of the world.

"Righteous Father, though the world does not know you, I know you, and they know that you have sent me. I have made you known to them, and will continue to make you known in order that the love you have for me may be in them and that I myself may be in them."

Matthew 26:36–46, Mark 14:32–42, Luke 22:40–46, John 18:1

When he had finished praying, Jesus left with his disciples and crossed the Kidron Valley. On the other side there was an olive grove, and he and his disciples went into it. Then Jesus went with his disciples to a place called Gethsemane, and he said to them, "Sit here while I go over there and pray." He took Peter, James and John, the two sons of Zebedee, along with him, and he began to be sorrowful and troubled. On reaching the place, he said to them, "Pray that you will not fall into temptation." Then he said to them, "My soul is overwhelmed with sorrow to the point of death. Stay here and keep watch with me."

He withdrew about a stone's throw beyond them, he fell with his face to the ground, knelt down and prayed that if possible the hour might pass from him. "*Abba*, my Father," he said, "if it is possible, may this cup be taken from me. Yet not as I will, but as you will."

Then he returned to his disciples and found them sleeping. "Simon," he said to Peter, "are you asleep? Could you not keep watch for one hour? Watch and pray so that you will not fall into temptation. The spirit is willing, but the body is weak."

He went away a second time and prayed, "My Father, if it is not possible for this cup to be taken away unless I drink it, may your will be done."

When he came back, he again found them sleeping, because their eyes were heavy. They did not know what to say to him. So he left them and went away once more and prayed the third time, saying the same thing. An angel from heaven appeared to him and strengthened him. And being in anguish, he prayed more earnestly, and his sweat was like drops of blood falling to the ground.

Returning the third time he found them asleep, exhausted from sorrow. He said to them, "Are you still sleeping and resting? Enough! Get up and pray so that you will not fall into temptation. The hour has come. Look, the Son of Man is betrayed into the hands of sinners. Rise! Let us go! Here comes my betrayer!" While he was still speaking a crowd came up, and the man who was called Judas, one of the Twelve, was leading them.

Matthew 26:47–50, Mark 14:43–46, Luke 22:47–48, John 18:2–9

Now Judas, one of the Twelve who betrayed him, knew the place, because Jesus had often met there with his disciples. So Judas came to the grove, guiding a detachment of soldiers and some officials from the chief priests, Pharisees, the teachers of the law and the elders of the people. Some in the crowd were carrying torches and lanterns, and they were armed with swords and clubs.

Jesus, knowing all that was going to happen to him, went out and asked them, "Who is it you want?"

"Jesus of Nazareth," they replied.

"I am he," Jesus said. (And Judas the traitor was standing there with them.) When Jesus said, "I am he," they drew back and fell to the ground.

Again he asked them, "Who is it you want?"

And they said, "Jesus of Nazareth."

"I told you that I am he," Jesus answered. "If you are looking for me, then let these men go." This happened so that the words he had spoken would be fulfilled: "I have not lost one of those you gave me."

Now the betrayer had arranged a signal with them: "The one I kiss is the man; arrest him and lead him away under guard." He approached Jesus to kiss him, but Jesus asked him, "Judas, are you betraying the Son of Man with a kiss?"

Judas said, "Greetings, Rabbi!" and kissed him.

Jesus replied, "Friend, do what you came for."

Then the men stepped forward, seized Jesus and arrested him.

Matthew 26:51–54, Mark 14:47, Luke 22:49–51, John 18:10–11

When Jesus' followers saw what was going to happen, they said, "Lord, should we strike with our swords?" One of Jesus' companions, Simon Peter, who had a sword, was standing near and reached for his sword. Peter drew it out and struck the servant of the high priest, cutting off his right ear. (The servant's name was Malchus.)

But Jesus answered, "No more of this!" He commanded Peter, "Put your sword back in its place," and said to him, "for all who draw the sword will die by the sword. Do you think I cannot call on my Father, and he will at once put at my disposal more than twelve legions of angels? But how then would the Scriptures be fulfilled that say it must happen in this way? Shall I not drink the cup the Father has given me?" And he touched the man's ear and healed him.

Matthew 26:55–56, Mark 14:48–50, Luke 22:52–54, John 18:12

Then Jesus said to the chief priests, the officers of the temple guard, and the elders, and the crowd who had come for him, "Am I leading a rebellion, that you have come with swords and clubs to capture me? Every day I sat in the temple courts teaching, and you did not lay a hand on me. But this is your hour—when darkness reigns. But this has all taken place that the writings of the prophets might be fulfilled." Then all the disciples deserted him and fled, and the detachment of soldiers with its commander and the Jewish officials arrested Jesus.

Summary

No moment in the life of Jesus is as thoroughly documented as the evening on which he was betrayed. This wealth of information is vital to understanding the meaning of the Lord's Supper, since every interpretation must return to this first observance as the test case for its soundness and trustworthiness. There are so many different modern-day traditions of observing the Lord's Supper—ranging from ornate to mundane, from frequent observance to seasonal or even annual celebration, from legalistic repetitiveness to indifference and even neglect. But on the night he was betrayed, Jesus himself presided over the table with his twelve apostles participating. It is here that the true purpose, meaning and effect of the Lord's Supper can be most fully appreciated. The better we understand the events of this evening, the more able we will be to fulfill Jesus' request to remember him in the manner he desires.

Notes

1. A chart explaining the compilation can be found in appendix 1, "A Chronological Narrative of the Lord's Supper."

2. Some would hesitate to approach the narrative in this way, since doing so seems to make Jesus repeat his predictions that one of his disciples would betray him and that the rest would deny him and scatter. Such repetition might be considered unusual, were it not recorded elsewhere in the Gospels that Jesus often repeated himself when teaching his disciples. For instance, in Mark and Luke, Jesus repeated the prediction of his suffering and death (Mark 8:31, 9:31, 10:33–34; Luke 9:44, 18:31–33). In the passage under consideration, both Matthew and Mark report that Jesus repeated his challenge to the disciples to stay awake while he prayed in the garden (Matthew—three times; Mark—two times). And in John's account of Jesus' appearance to a group of disciples not long after his resurrection, Jesus repeated himself three times when he asked Peter if he truly loved him (John 21:15ff). In light of how poorly the disciples understood the purposes of Jesus, and in view of their failure to grasp the events that ensued on that very evening, the probability of repetition on this particular occasion is as high as ever.

3. "After the supper" is translated "after they had eaten" in the NASB.

4

Shadows and Realities

G od could have freed the Israelites from the bondage of Egypt with any miraculous sign he wanted, but he purposefully chose the death of the firstborn and the Passover celebration because of his foreordained plan of salvation for mankind:

> For you know that it was not with perishable things such as silver or gold that you were redeemed from the empty way of life handed down to you from your forefathers, but with the precious blood of Christ, a lamb without blemish or defect. He was chosen before the creation of the world, but was revealed in these last times for your sake. Through him you believe in God, who raised him from the dead and glorified him, and so your faith and hope are in God. (1 Peter 1:18–21)

All the prescribed sacrifices of the Law, along with its food regulations and religious holidays, were a "shadow of the things that were to come; the reality, however, is found in Christ" (Colossians 2:17). Although the stated purpose of keeping the Passover was commemorative of the deliverance of the Israelites, the details behind the historic event were orchestrated by God to foreshadow the coming sacrifice of Jesus Christ.

The Passover Lamb

The evening Jesus was betrayed was not the first time he chose the Passover as an occasion to reveal something about himself or the nature of his mission. When he was just twelve years old, Jesus' parents took him up to Jerusalem for the Passover. It was there he revealed the nature of his relationship to God by the question, "Didn't you know I had to be in my

Father's house?" (Luke 2:49). Many years later, he returned to Jerusalem just before the Passover and cleared the temple, rebuking them for turning his Father's house into "a market" (John 2:16). On that occasion, Jesus also predicted his own resurrection by saying that he would "destroy this temple" (his body) and in three days raise it up again (John 2:19–21). This reminded his disciples of Psalm 69, which also contained prophetic detail of the crucifixion. And just before another Passover, Jesus fed the five thousand (John 6)—the only miracle recorded in every Gospel—and taught that those who would truly have life must eat his flesh and drink his blood. He then predicted that he would be betrayed by one of the Twelve. This overview highlights a very interesting aspect of the Gospel of John: more than half of its narrative takes place within a few days of various Passover feasts during the lifetime of Jesus (John 2:13–25, 6:1–71, 11:55–20:23). For John, there was a deep connection between the meaning of the Passover and the good news about Jesus Christ.

John introduces us to Jesus in his Gospel with the testimony of John the Baptist: "Look, the Lamb of God who takes away the sin of the world!" (John 1:29). The identification of Jesus as the Lamb of God was again confirmed in his death. Although Pilate ordered that his legs be broken to ensure death, the soldiers found this unnecessary, because Jesus was already dead—thus fulfilling the regulation that no bone of the Passover lamb be broken (John 19:31–37; see Exodus 12:46, Numbers 9:12). Throughout his adult life, celebrating the Passover must have been an intensely emotional experience for Jesus, for he was fully aware that the true Passover lamb had come into the world and had yet to be killed. In the book of Revelation, Jesus is described as the Lamb that was slain and yet lived (5:6), the only one worthy to open the scroll (5:9). It was the Lamb's blood that washed the saints' robes and made them white (7:14), and the church—the New Jerusalem (21:2)—is described as the wife of the Lamb (19:7).

Other New Testament writers also testified that the preparation and consumption of the Passover lamb foreshadowed specific details of the sacrifice of Jesus Christ:

1) The Passover lamb needed to be a year-old male lamb without defect; Jesus was holy, blameless, pure and set apart from sinners (Exodus 12:5, Hebrews 7:26).
2) The blood of the Passover lamb was to be sprinkled on the doorposts and lintels (a beam set upon two posts) as a sign for the death angel to pass over and spare the household; the blood of Jesus was shed on the cross (a beam set on a single post) to reconcile all things to God and save the household of God from condemnation (Exodus 12:7, Colossians 1:20, Hebrews 12:24).

Some of the Passover regulations also find their counterpart in the establishment of the Lord's Supper:

3) The first Passover was celebrated by household, with the head of each household responsible for the sacrificial lamb; the first celebration of the Lord's Supper was by Jesus and his disciples (his spiritual household, Mark 3:34–35), and as the head of the household, Jesus provided the lamb for the sacrifice by offering himself (Exodus 12:3, Matthew 26:20ff).
4) The Passover celebration was to be repeated annually and its meaning was to be explained to the children; Jesus asked his disciples to eat the bread and drink the cup in memory of him and thus proclaim his death until he comes (Exodus 12:26–27, 1 Corinthians 11:24–26).

And even the "passing over" by the death angel and the exodus out of Egypt find significant parallels in Christ's sacrifice:

5) Freeing the people of Israel from their bondage required the death of the firstborn of Egypt; freeing us from our sins required the death of God's firstborn (Exodus 12:29–32, Revelation 1:5).

6) The "rescued" firstborn of Israel were later redeemed by God through the setting apart of the tribe of Levi (including the descendants of Aaron) as priests; the blood of Christ purchased men for God from all nations to be a kingdom and priests to serve God and reign on earth (Numbers 3:12–13, Revelation 5:9–10).

7) Moses was a faithful servant in God's house leading the people of Israel; Jesus is a faithful son in God's house leading us if we hold on to our courage and the hope of which we boast (Hebrews 3:5–6).

It should not surprise us that the focus of the evening on which Jesus was betrayed was *not* the Jewish Passover; for the true Passover lamb had come into the world and was about to be offered to fulfill God's eternal purposes.

The Bread and the Cup

Having taken a panoramic view of the last evening of Jesus' life in the previous chapter, it is also helpful to closely examine those few verses that actually describe the institution of the Lord's Supper: Matthew 26:26–29, Mark 14:22–25 and Luke 22:19–20. From these passages we can derive a "short text" in which only common words and phrases are included, and also a "long text" in which all words and phrases are compiled.[1] The short text emphasizes the bare essence of the events, while the longer text paints a more detailed picture.

Short Text

> Jesus took bread, gave thanks and broke it, and gave it to his disciples, saying, "This is my body." Then he took the cup. "This is my blood of the covenant, which is poured out for many."

Long Text

> And while they were eating, Jesus took bread, gave thanks and broke it, and gave it to his disciples, saying, "Take it and eat; this is my body given for you; do this in remembrance of me."

Then, in the same way after the supper, he took the cup, gave thanks and offered it to them, saying, "Drink from it, all of you." And they all drank from it. "This is my blood of the [new] covenant,[a] which is poured out for many[b] for the forgiveness of sins," he said to them. "I tell you the truth, I will not drink again of the fruit of the vine until that day when I drink it anew in my Father's kingdom."[c]

Variant Readings

[a] "This is my blood of the [new] covenant" (Matthew, Mark) "This cup is the new covenant in my blood" (Luke); [new] some manuscripts;

[b] "for many" (Matthew, Mark) / "for you" (Luke);

[c] "anew in my Father's kingdom" (Matthew) / "in the kingdom of God" (Mark)

Considering all the details recorded in the Gospels concerning the night of Jesus' betrayal, one point becomes very clear: Jesus intended for the Lord's Supper to be simple and practical. He selected two elements from the table before him that were universal in his day—bread and wine.[2] He then presented these to his disciples and asked them to imitate his example by breaking the bread and sharing the cup together, thus remembering his offered body and his blood of the new covenant. This commemorative meal was not simply meant to honor the deeds that Jesus was about to perform, but to remind them who his sacrifice was for: "for many," and more specifically, "for you." The Lord's Supper is intended to make the participant reflect not only on what Jesus accomplished through his sacrifice, but also on what the participant has done to make Christ's sacrifice necessary.

'This Is My Body'

The bread reminds us of the sacrifice of Christ's body. It was blessed, broken and given. In the Gospels the word "body" is used exclusively in a literal, physical sense—the earthly dwelling of the spirit.[3] Jesus demonstrated this concept by referring to his own physical body when stating that he would "destroy this temple, and...raise it again in three days" (John

2:19). The physical body of Jesus was a temple wherein resided the only begotten Son of God. Consider the following scriptures that explain the significance of Christ's physical body:

> Once you were alienated from God and were enemies in your minds because of your evil behavior. But now he has reconciled you by Christ's physical body through death to present you holy in his sight, without blemish and free from accusation—if you continue in your faith, established and firm, not moved from the hope held out in the gospel. (Colossians 1:21–23)

> The law is only a shadow of the good things that are coming—not the realities themselves. For this reason it can never, by the same sacrifices repeated endlessly year after year, make perfect those who draw near to worship. …But those sacrifices are an annual reminder of sins, because it is impossible for the blood of bulls and goats to take away sins.
>
> Therefore, when Christ came into the world, he said:
>
> > "Sacrifice and offering you did not desire,
> >> but a body you prepared for me;
> > with burnt offerings and sin offerings
> >> you were not pleased.
> > Then I said, 'Here I am—it is written about me in the
> >> scroll—
> > I have come to do your will, O God.'"
>
> …He sets aside the first to establish the second. And by that will, we have been made holy through the sacrifice of the body of Jesus Christ once for all. (Hebrews 10:1–10, including a quote from Psalm 40:6–8)

> To this you were called, because Christ suffered for you, leaving you an example, that you should follow in his steps.
>
> > "He committed no sin,
> >> and no deceit was found in his mouth."
>
> When they hurled their insults at him, he did not retaliate; when he suffered, he made no threats. Instead, he entrusted himself to him who judges justly. He himself bore our sins in

his body on the tree, so that we might die to sins and live
for righteousness; by his wounds you have been healed.
(1 Peter 2:21–24, including a quote from Isaiah 53:9)

Whenever the physical body of Christ is mentioned, the message is clear: the only begotten Son of God took human form and gave up the power and position of Godhood.

The Word became flesh and made his dwelling among us.
We have seen his glory, the glory of the One and Only, who
came from the Father, full of grace and truth. (John 1:14)

The sacrifice of Jesus began long before his death on the cross. His presence in a human body already implied that he had given up the glory he had earlier shared with his Father in heaven (John 17:4–5).

Christ Jesus...being in very nature God,
    did not consider equality with God something to be
        grasped,
but made himself nothing,
    taking the very nature of a servant,
    being made in human likeness.
And being found in appearance as a man
    he humbled himself
    and became obedient to death—
        even death on a cross! (Philippians 2:6–8)

Although no human being can truly appreciate the meaning of Christ's sacrifice of giving up equality with God, the obedience he demonstrated in his physical body rendered his humility completely understandable to each one of us. It was no easier for Jesus to sacrifice his physical life in obedience to God than for any other man. As Jesus witnessed his disciples struggle unsuccessfully to simply keep watch and pray with him in the Garden of Gethsemane, he told them, "The spirit is willing, but the flesh is weak" (Mark 14:38). Jesus felt and understood their weakness since he shared in their humanity (Hebrews 2:14, 18). With regard to his own body, Jesus' death on the cross would truly be a living sacrifice that would require conscious decision and the complete submission of his will until the moment of its completion. Through obedience the sacrifice of Jesus' body was made perfect, and he became the source of eternal life for all who obey him (Hebrews 5:9). For Jesus the weakness of the flesh was not an excuse for sin, but an opportunity for bringing glory to God through obedience and righteousness. Jesus chose the bread of the Lord's Supper to remind us that the Son of God took on a physical body and truly became flesh like each one of us—to the point that he bore our sins in his body on the cross.

'This Is My Blood'

The cup reminds us of the blood of the new covenant, a statement of God's heart toward mankind: it was "poured out for many." With these words Jesus shows that he was establishing a new covenant, paralleling the words of Moses that had ratified the first covenant:

> Moses then took the blood, sprinkled it on the people and said, "This is the blood of the covenant that the LORD has made with you in accordance with all these words." (Exodus 24:8)

Under the old covenant, blood was used to make things holy. Its effect, however, was merely external and momentary. The effect of Jesus' blood lasts forever. Consider the following scriptures:

> For you know that it was not with perishable things such as silver or gold that you were redeemed from the empty way of life handed down to you from your forefathers, but with the precious blood of Christ, a lamb without blemish or defect. (1 Peter 1:18–19)

> God was pleased to have all his fullness dwell in him, and through him to reconcile to himself all things, whether things on earth or things in heaven, by making peace through his blood, shed on the cross. (Colossians 1:19–20)

> The blood of goats and bulls and the ashes of a heifer sprinkled on those who are ceremonially unclean sanctify them so that they are outwardly clean. How much more, then, will the blood of Christ, who through the eternal Spirit

offered himself unblemished to God, cleanse our consciences from acts that lead to death, so that we may serve
the living God!

For this reason Christ is the mediator of a new covenant,
that those who are called may receive the promised eternal
inheritance—now that he has died as a ransom to set them
free from the sins committed under the first covenant.

…A will is in force only when somebody has died; it never
takes effect while the one who made it is living. This is why
even the first covenant was not put into effect without
blood.…The law requires that nearly everything be cleansed
with blood, and without the shedding of blood there is no
forgiveness. (Hebrews 9:13–22)

The blood of Jesus is the currency of our salvation—it pays
the ransom for our freedom from sin and corruption. It is the
agent of our cleansing, bringing us into contact with God's
mercy and forgiveness. The offering of Christ's blood makes
peace between God and man. The Old Testament very clearly
lays out this principle:

For the life of a creature is in the blood, and I have given it to
you to make atonement for yourselves on the altar; it is the
blood that makes atonement for one's life. (Leviticus 17:11)

Our sins demand retribution, and only the payment of
Christ's life—through his blood—can buy back our lives. Jesus
taught his disciples that

"The Son of Man did not come to be served, but to serve,
and to give his life as a ransom for many." (Matthew 20:28,
Mark 10:45)

Jesus used the cup of the Lord's Supper to remind us of God's
plan of redemption. Through the shedding of his blood, the new
covenant was activated and empowered to offer forgiveness,
redemption and sanctification to all those who would accept it.

Outside the Camp

For those who were familiar with the sacrifices prescribed by
the Mosaic Law, this differentiation between body and blood

was nothing new. Specific details about what was to be done with the body and blood of various offerings demonstrate subtle differences in meaning between each type of sacrifice. Depending upon the occasion, the body (i.e., meat, fat, hide) of the sacrifice was to be completely consumed by fire; or, if only partially consumed, the remainder was to be eaten by the priest or by the one making the sacrifice or by both of them. The blood of the sacrifice was either consumed by fire, ceremonially poured out or sprinkled on specific objects or areas of worship to make them holy. Although the circumstance and context of the Lord's Supper readily connects our thoughts to the Passover celebration, the specific effects of the sacrifice of Christ's body and blood reminds us of yet another annual celebration of the Mosaic Law: the Day of Atonement.

According to the Law of Moses (Leviticus 16:1ff), the sacrifices of the Day of Atonement were to include two special sin offerings made by the high priest: a bull for his own sins and a goat for the sins of the people. Typically, sin offerings were slaughtered, some blood smeared on the horns of the altar of burnt offering at the entrance of the Tent of Meeting, and the rest of the blood poured out on the base of the altar. The fat surrounding the inner parts of these offerings was also burned on the altar. The meat of the sacrifice was then given to the priests to be eaten in a holy place, except when the sin offerings had been made for the sake of a priest or the whole community— which required that the bodies be taken outside the camp and burned. This exception involving the general sin offerings made for the high priest and the people agrees with the instructions concerning the sin offerings made on the Day of Atonement that were specifically for the high priest and for the people. The sacrificed bodies of both the bull and the goat were taken outside the camp and burned.

Unique to the Day of Atonement, the blood of these sacrifices was not poured out on the base of the altar. After filling a censer with burning coals from the altar of incense, the high priest was to enter the Most Holy Place. There, he would add incense to the fire and then sprinkle the bull's blood on the front of the atonement cover and before it. He then was to repeat this process with the goat's blood. Then he would return to the altar of incense and take some of the bull's blood and some of the goat's blood and put it on the horns of the altar. These sacrifices not only atoned for the sins of the high priest and the people, but they made atonement for the Most Holy Place, the Tent of Meeting and the altar of incense.

As in the case of the Passover celebration, these instructions and regulations were a foreshadowing of the reality that would be revealed in Jesus Christ:

> The high priest carries the blood of animals into the Most Holy Place as a sin offering, but the bodies are burned outside the camp. And so Jesus also suffered outside the city gate to make the people holy through his own blood. Let us, then, go to him outside the camp, bearing the disgrace he bore. (Hebrews 13:11–13)

Therefore, according to the Law, the same sacrifice that yielded blood worthy of being taken into the Most Holy Place to make atonement for sins left a body that needed to be taken outside the camp and burned. The reality that stands behind this dichotomy helps better explain the agony that Jesus endured in the Garden of Gethsemane as he anticipated his crucifixion. Although the blood of his sacrifice would produce the most powerful cleansing agent of all time and would be the source of man's salvation, his body would bear the shame, disgrace and curse of death on a cross.

Bearing the Sins of the World

If there ever was a "God forsaken" place on earth, it was the cross of Jesus Christ. The path to the cross was lined with betrayal, desertion and false accusation involving even the closest friends of Jesus. The very laws of God that were meant to delight, sustain and bring justice to his chosen people were invoked against the only begotten Son to wrongly condemn him to death. Even God the Father—the great defender of the poor, the widow and the orphan—did not immediately respond to the cries and tears of Jesus. Rather, he painfully endured Jesus' pleas and allowed sin and condemnation to finish their work to the point of death. Jesus' perfect and sinless life on earth ended in indignity, injustice and loneliness on the cross.

As already noted, the annual Passover celebration was rich with meaning for the Israelites because of the way that God had orchestrated the events surrounding their deliverance out of Egypt. By contrast, the law requiring the bodies of sin offerings that had been made for the high priest and the people to be taken outside the camp and burned—not simply consumed by fire or eaten by the priests—remained a mystery until the reality was revealed in the death of Jesus Christ. For the Jewish mind, the idea of anything being banished to a place outside the camp carried with it the stigma of condemnation and uncleanness. According to the Law, blasphemers and Sabbath-breakers were to be taken outside the camp and stoned to death (Leviticus 24:14, 23; Numbers 15:35, 36); Jesus was falsely accused of both of these trespasses by the Jewish authorities of his day (Mark 14:63, 64; John 5:18). The Law required that anyone who had an infectious skin disease, a discharge of any kind or who was ceremonially unclean because of contact with a dead body should to be sent outside the camp to maintain "cleanness" in the camp (Numbers 5:3–4, Isaiah 53:4). Throughout his life, Jesus touched both the dead and the leprous, and they were raised back to life or had their flesh restored to health. Spiritually speaking, Jesus took up our infirmities, carried our diseases (i.e., bore our sin and condemnation) and suffered outside the city gates (Matthew 8:18, Hebrews 13:12). Although the Law was wrongly applied to condemn Jesus as guilty of a capital offense, in the end the Law condemned Jesus through the simple principle that anyone who is hung on a tree is under God's curse (Deuteronomy 21:23). Jesus redeemed us from the curse of the law by becoming a curse for us (Galatians 3:13):

God made him who had no sin to be sin for us, so that in him we might become the righteousness of God. (2 Corinthians 5:21)

Jesus didn't simply bear our sins by some simple trick of semantics or play on words—he took the guilt of our sins upon himself and bore the result of our condemnation. As surely as sinful mankind is declared righteous as a result of his sacrifice, Jesus assumed the weight of mankind's sin through his death on the cross—thus requiring his banishment.

The truth that Jesus took the sins of the world upon himself on the cross is confirmed by events subsequent to his death. After rising from the dead on the first day of the week, Jesus first revealed himself to Mary Magdalene and said, "Do not hold on to me, for I have not yet returned to the Father. Go instead to my brothers and tell them, 'I am returning to my Father and your Father, to my God and your God'" (John 20:17). The fact that Jesus had not yet returned to his Father in heaven proves that the fate of all sinful men had overtaken him: he had descended into Hades, the waiting place for judgment for the departed souls of men. Peter attested to this situation in his first public sermon after the resurrection by quoting a psalm of David:

"But God raised him from the dead, freeing him from the agony of death, because it was impossible for death to keep its hold on him. David said about him:

"'I saw the Lord always before me.
  Because he is at my right hand,
  I will not be shaken.
Therefore my heart is glad and my tongue rejoices;
  my body also will live in hope,
because you will not abandon me to the grave [Hades],
  nor will you let your Holy One see decay.
You have made known to me the paths of life;
  you will fill me with joy in your presence.'

"Brothers, I can tell you confidently that the patriarch David died and was buried, and his tomb is here to this day. But he was a prophet and knew that God had promised him on oath

> that he would place one of his descendants on his throne. Seeing what was ahead, he spoke of the resurrection of the Christ, that he was not abandoned to the grave [Hades], nor did his body see decay. God has raised this Jesus to life, and we are all witnesses of the fact." (Acts 2:24–32, including a quote from Psalm 16:8–11)

Although Jesus died and went to Hades just as any other man would, God rescued him and raised him to life again. Just as Jesus had predicted to his disciples, the gates of Hades would not overcome his kingdom (Matthew 16:18).

The foreshadowing of the sin offerings on the Day of Atonement provides us with insight into the resurrection of Jesus—his own salvation from death. If the sacrifice of Jesus would cover our sins and save us from condemnation, what sacrifice would in turn cover the sinfulness he assimilated on our behalf? The Law required that the high priest offer a sin offering not only for the people, but also for himself (Leviticus 16:1ff). Although Jesus completely bore our sins on the cross and received our condemnation in his body, the perfect sacrifice of his blood, brought into the true Most Holy Place in heaven, bought forgiveness and redemption even for God's high priest:

> If perfection could have been attained through the Levitical priesthood (for on the basis of it the law was given to the people), why was there still need for another priest to come?…one who has become a priest not on the basis of a regulation as to his ancestry but on the basis of the power of an indestructible life.…The former regulation is set aside because it was weak and useless (for the law made nothing perfect), and a better hope is introduced, by which we draw near to God. (Hebrews 7:11, 16, 18–19)

Truly the perfect sacrifice was one that covered not only the sins of the people but the sins of the high priest as well. Although Jesus bore our sins and the consequence of our condemnation, the sacrifice of his blood provided salvation for him as well.

> For what the law was powerless to do in that it was weakened by the sinful nature, God did by sending his own Son in the likeness of sinful man to be a sin offering. And so he condemned sin in sinful man, in order that the righteous requirements of the law might be fully met in us, who do not live according to the sinful nature but according to the Spirit. (Romans 8:3–4)

The sin offerings of the Day of Atonement foreshadowed the reality of the crucifixion of Jesus Christ. While Jesus bore the guilt of our sins in his body and suffered outside the camp like a criminal or an unclean person, his blood became the perfect sacrifice—worthy of being offered before the very throne of God in heaven—for the sins of all men.

The New Covenant

Compared to the splendor of the temple and all the pomp and regulation of the annual festivals, the Lord's Supper is strikingly straightforward and ordinary. For the first disciples, it must have been almost unbelievable that participation in this simple memorial meal would be the only commemorative act that Jesus would command his followers to do. It would take a few years for the disciples of Jesus to actually grasp this truth, since the idea of breaking from mainstream Judaism in matters of temple worship (Acts 3:1) and ceremonial cleanness (Acts 10:14) was not immediately understood—even by Peter, who was one of the original Twelve. From the inception of the new covenant, God clearly wanted to emphasize how much it differed from the old. While the Israelites had been physically delivered from bondage in Egypt, the people of this new covenant would be delivered from bondage to sin and guilt. The old covenant had been written on tablets of stone, but the new covenant would be written on the "tablets of human hearts" (2 Corinthians 3:3). The promises of the old covenant focused on physical blessings and an earthly promised land, but the new covenant would focus on spiritual blessings and an inheritance in heaven. The Hebrew writer makes it clear that the people of this new covenant have a spiritual connection to God based on complete forgiveness and the presence of the law in their hearts:

> But the ministry Jesus has received is as superior to theirs as the covenant of which he is mediator is superior to the old one, and it is founded on better promises.
>
> For if there had been nothing wrong with that first covenant, no place would have been sought for another. But God found fault with the people and said:
>
> > "The time is coming, declares the Lord,
> >   when I will make a new covenant
> > with the house of Israel
> >   and with the house of Judah.
> > It will not be like the covenant
> >   I made with their forefathers
> > when I took them by the hand
> >   to lead them out of Egypt,
> > because they did not remain faithful to my covenant,
> >   and I turned away from them,
> >   declares the Lord.
> > This is the covenant I will make with the house of Israel
> >   after that time, declares the Lord.
> > I will put my laws in their minds
> >   and write them on their hearts.
> > I will be their God,
> >   and they will be my people.
> > No longer will a man teach his neighbor,
> >   or a man his brother, saying, 'Know the Lord,'
> > because they will all know me,
> >   from the least of them to the greatest.
> > For I will forgive their wickedness
> >   and will remember their sins no more."
>
> By calling this covenant "new," he has made the first one obsolete; and what is obsolete and aging will soon disappear. (Hebrews 8:6–13)

This new covenant was fundamentally different from the old covenant, and the modesty and simplicity of the Lord's Supper represent quite a contrast to the elaborate nature of the Jewish feasts.

Summary

The prophetic details of the Old Testament are found in more than just the direct words of prophecy that God spoke through his prophets. A powerful foreshadowing of future events and spiritual truths can also be seen in God's direct intervention in the affairs of men. Within the Mosaic system of food laws, sacrifice and religious festivals, we can see glimpses of the future reality of Christ's sacrifice. The Gospel of John clearly confirms the identity of Jesus as the ultimate Passover lamb of God who came to take away the sins of the world (John 1:29–35, 19:36). As discussed in chapter 1, the Passover lamb was the only regular sacrifice that predated the giving of the Law and the establishment of the Levitical priesthood. The unique historical position occupied by the Passover sacrifice allowed it to define the fundamental principle of redemption through the offering of a lamb in place of the firstborn of Israel. As a result, redemption through sacrifice became the basis for the whole Mosaic system of worship and atonement. God allowed the Israelites to make atonement for their lives through the sacrifice (sin and guilt offerings) of blood (that is, the giving of another life). God also used the principle of redemption of the firstborn when he set apart the Levites to do the work at the Tent of Meeting on behalf of all the Israelites. With the sacrifice of his Son, God took this message of deliverance to its highest level as he once and for all provided for the redemption of all his children from the bondage of sin and death. On the basis of Jesus' sacrifice, God set apart for himself "a chosen people, a royal priesthood, a holy nation, a people belonging to [him]" (1 Peter 2:9). During the last Passover celebration of his life, Jesus instituted a memorial for this new covenant between God and his people that would be based upon the sacrifice of his body and blood.

Considering the significance of this event and the length of time that Israel had waited for the new covenant to be established, this new memorial feast was remarkably simple. Making use of the bread and wine already at hand, "Jesus took bread, gave thanks and broke it, and gave it to his disciples, saying, 'This is my body.' He took the cup and said, 'This is my blood of the covenant, which is poured out for many'" (Short Text). The bread represented the body of Jesus, which was the vessel of his physical life on earth. Jesus willingly sacrificed his body on the cross, and it was there that his body also became the vessel for the guilt of the sins of all men. The fruit of the vine represented the blood of Jesus that redeems us from death and cleanses our consciences before God—it was the only sacrifice that could be considered worthy of paying for our salvation. As one might expect from men caught up in a dizzying array of events, deep insight into the purposes of Jesus eluded the disciples that evening. It was only after his resurrection that they began to fully understand the implications of the memorial supper they had shared together.

Another annual Jewish festival that provides rich insight into the sacrifice of Jesus Christ is the Day of Atonement. The fact that the blood of the sin offerings would be taken into the Most Holy Place and that the body would be disposed of outside the camp showed the paradox of Christ's matchless sacrifice. To provide us with mercy, Jesus had to submit to absolute injustice. In order for men to be declared "truly" righteous, Jesus needed to "truly" take the sin of all men upon himself. For us, the cross is our place of hope and redemption; but for Jesus, it was the place where he was forsaken by God. "Jesus suffered outside the city gate to make the people holy through his blood" (Hebrews 13:12). The law was a shadow of the things that were to come; the reality, however, is found in Christ" (Colossians 2:17).

Notes

1. See appendix 2 "A Conflated Narrative of the Lord's Supper."

2. Bread and wine were common, not only at Passover meals, but also at every meal in that culture. John F. Walvoord, and Roy B. Zuck, *The Bible Knowledge Commentary,* (Wheaton, Ill.: Scripture Press Publications, Inc., 1983, 1985), s.v. "Luke 22:14–20." Although the bread that Jesus used was most definitely *unleavened* since it was the time of the Passover and the Feast of Unleavened Bread, neither Jesus nor the New Testament writers emphasized this characteristic or made it a clear stipulation for the Lord's Supper—Jesus simply used the bread that was at hand on the table before him. In the same way, we assume that the cup that Jesus shared most likely contained wine mixed with water (some alcoholic content), since that was the standard custom of the time, but again the words of Jesus and the apostles only affirm that it was a product of the grapevine: "the fruit of the vine."

3. The pairing of "body and blood" in the Lord's Supper, instead of the more common Greek pairing of "flesh and blood," is worthy of attention. The most satisfactory explanation is that the New Testament writers were challenged by the same situation that had earlier confronted the translators of the Septuagint, namely, that the Hebrew and Aramaic languages have just one word for "flesh" and "(living) body," whereas the Greek language has two. The Greek word for "flesh" (*sarx*) focuses on the actual "substance" of the body, whereas the Greek word for "body" (*soma*) focuses more on the "vessel of the spirit" and "instrument of life." By the fourth and third centuries BC, the word "body" was already beginning to have the secondary meaning of a "group of people" in Greek thought. This semantic development would later prove useful for describing Christ's relationship to the church. Additionally, "flesh" in Greek was often used in opposition to "spirit" (*pneuma*) to refer to human life and its desires apart from God. The "works of the flesh" (Galatians 5:19, KJV; "acts of the sinful nature," NIV) are what man, left to himself, is capable of producing. In the passages of the New Testament that make a direct reference to the Lord's Supper, the pairing of "body and blood" is always found.

5

The Power of the Lord's Supper

The Lord's Supper was meant to be simple, practical and powerful. With two ordinary elements, bread and fruit of the vine, Jesus shared a special moment with his closest disciples and asked them to meditate on the sacrifice of his physical life and the new covenant that his blood established. The atmosphere of the celebration was not pretentious, arrogant or even religious; instead, there was a deep sense of family, honesty and genuine love on the part of Jesus. Fully aware of the human tendency to focus on the outward appearance of things and lose sight of their spiritual value and significance, Jesus asked his disciples to observe this emblematic Supper in remembrance of him. The bread and the cup were to be tangible reminders that the Son of God willingly gave over his life into the hands of sinful men, and that although our sin put him to death on the cross, it was the purpose of God to redeem us through the sacrifice of his blood.

The Passover Connection

If not for the fact that the Gospel writers introduce the last evening of Jesus' life with the sending of his disciples to make preparations for the Passover (actually referred to as the "first day of the Feast of Unleavened Bread"), it might not even be clear that this was, in fact, the context for their gathering in the upper room. None of the Gospel writers seems to emphasize the details of celebrating the Passover. For example, reference is made to unleavened bread being present on the table, but there is no mention of "bitter herbs," although the dipping of the bread into the dish may have implied its presence. Furthermore, there is no reference made to eating the "sacrificial lamb,"[1] and no record of recounting Israel's deliverance from Egypt or the traditional dialogue between father and son. Although it would only be reasonable to assume that Jesus and the apostles followed all of the regulations surrounding the Passover, reporting the faithful adherence to these regulations was not the focus of the Gospel writers.

Evidence that the Passover was in fact celebrated comes more from certain details reflective of Jewish customs of the day—such as reclining at the table, using multiple cups of wine, calling the wine the "fruit of the vine" and singing a closing hymn. We can conclude that the Lord's Supper did more than simply modify the Passover celebration and incorporate all of its customs and regulations. Although Jesus clearly chose the context of the Passover feast as the setting for the first observance of the Lord's Supper (a celebration within a celebration on that particular evening)— we have no indication that any attempt was made to associate those rules with the new ordinance. Therefore we have no reason to assume that the regulations pertaining to the Passover— whether from the Old Testament or the Jewish tradition of that period—were to be preserved in the celebration of the Lord's Supper.

Instead of focusing on the formal Passover celebration, Jesus devoted the evening to teaching and prayer. He repeatedly predicted to his disciples that one of them would betray him, all of them would be scattered and he himself would soon suffer and die. He tried to get them to understand that to be his disciples meant that they must not only imitate his heart to serve, but also be ready for the advent of trials similar to his in their own lives. He went on to explain that one of the benefits of his return to the Father would be that the Holy Spirit would come and help them, even indwell them. Finally, he prayed very specifically that he would fulfill God's will, and he also prayed for the future success of his disciples, that they would be unified and follow his example of submission to God.

While the actual celebration of the Lord's Supper was just a small part of what took place that evening, it truly captured the essence of what Jesus was trying to teach his disciples. He was not simply a rabbi seeking to influence the thinking of his followers; he was calling them to a level of imitation that could in fact be considered *participation* in his very life. The ultimate test of being a disciple of Jesus is not just agreement with his teaching, but wholehearted implementation of his principles in how we think and make our decisions—even to the point of sacrificing our very lives. The Lord's Supper was not connected to the Passover observance by ritual or regulation, but by the common theme of remembering God's deliverance in the lives of his people.

Effects of Participating

Insight into the nature of the Lord's Supper can be gained by examining the way in which the evening concluded for those who had participated in its first celebration. For Jesus, the events of that evening worked to strengthen his resolve to do his Father's will. After the Supper, he wrestled with God's will in prayer in Gethsemane and completely accepted the cup of suffering that he was given to drink. For the disciples, their participation in the Lord's Supper had a short-lived spiritual effect: they went from questioning each other about who was the worst (the predicted betrayer) to arguing about who was the greatest (Luke 22:22–24). The disciples' resolve to participate in Christ's sacrifice was so weak that they were not even able to stay awake with Jesus during his time of struggle in prayer in the garden. Consequently, they were not ready to stand the test of their convictions.

At the moment of Jesus' arrest, eleven of them deserted the Lord and fled. For the twelfth, Judas, it would be the most tragic night of his life, as he followed through with his plan to betray the Son of God into the hands of unrighteous men. Judas not only participated in the Lord's Supper together with the other disciples (Luke 22:21), but Jesus washed his feet along with theirs. Jesus knew exactly what was about to happen, but the other disciples did not understand that Judas was the betrayer, nor did they comprehend Jesus' words that sent Judas on his way to fulfill his wicked scheme (John 13:26–30).

By examining these clearly different outcomes in the lives of those who shared in its first observance, we can determine some fundamental truths about the effect of participation in the Lord's Supper. First, the effectiveness of the Lord's Supper in strengthening and building up an individual is totally dependent on that person's acceptance and understanding of the meaning of the bread and the fruit of the vine. Second, there is nothing magical or mystical in the physical elements of the Lord's Supper, even after being blessed by Jesus himself. The blessed bread and cup did not possess some sort of power to automatically change the character or heart of a participant. Third, a lack of spirituality on the part of one participant does not invalidate the experience for others who participate.

The superficiality of those who treated the Lord's Supper lightly and did not use the opportunity to focus on the example and heart of Jesus is demonstrated through their subsequent weakness and inability to withstand the testing of their faith. The Lord's Supper was meant to be commemorative of Christ's life, and its effect and operation depends totally on the individual understanding of its participants as to the character of Christ and the nature of his sacrifice. The Hebrew writer sums this up beautifully:

> Let us fix our eyes on Jesus, the author and perfecter of our faith, who for the joy set before him endured the cross, scorning its shame, and sat down at the right hand of the throne of God. Consider him who endured such opposition from sinful men, so that you will not grow weary and lose heart. (Hebrews 12:2–3)

Misconceptions

Many of the misconceptions surrounding the Lord's Supper seem to stem from both conscious and unconscious associations made with the Passover celebration. Historically, there have been numerous attempts to institutionalize Christianity and ritualize the teachings of the New Testament in a way that would make God's people more like an "earthly" nation than the spiritual nation that Jesus intended. In other words, contrary to the teachings of the apostles—which sought to free people from legalistic adherence to external regulations, including the Law of Moses—there has been a tendency to revert to an Old Testament model for God's people—complete with physical territory, political power, ritual ceremonies, clergy-laity distinctions and special holy places of worship. As a result of such tendencies, participation in the Lord's Supper did not long remain an issue of simply *remembering* Jesus. It also became a test of fellowship and a sign of God's approval among those professing to be followers of Jesus Christ.

Any explanation as to the purpose, meaning and effect of the Lord's Supper must return to this first celebration as its point of reference. Since Jesus himself presided over the table and his twelve apostles participated, it is here that the purposes and even limitations of the memorial meal can best be understood. The record of this initial celebration will either validate or discredit any current understanding or practice. Many common misconceptions can be laid to rest by simple comparison to the first celebration of the Lord's Supper.

One such misconception is that the Lord's Supper was intended to be the Passover "equivalent" of the New Testament and has thereby inherited the stringent rules and formality of this Old Testament celebration. There is no evidence from the Gospel accounts that Jesus was trying to officially associate the Lord's Supper with the Passover in any way. In fact, we see more evidence of following contemporary Jewish customs than of compliance to the Mosaic ordinances. Although the Lord's Supper shares a few similarities in form with the Passover (it was a memorial feast and one of the elements was unleavened bread), there are many significant differences:

- The first observance of the Passover was an actual participation in God's plan of physically "saving" the Israelites. If they did not follow God's instructions

exactly, their firstborn would literally be killed.
Afterward, the Passover was to be celebrated annually
in commemoration of Israel's redemption. The Lord's
Supper, on the other hand, was a memorial meal from
its inception, having no attendant physical consequences associated with its first celebration. There
were, however, spiritual consequences of not participating with the right heart and attitude.

- The Passover celebration was a well-defined ceremony
  with detailed directions recorded in more than seventy
  verses of Scripture. By the time of the first century, the
  Passover celebration had become even more complex
  due to the addition of various man-made traditions. By
  contrast, the instructions concerning the institution of the
  Lord's Supper were very simple and to the point. It was a
  symbolic meal of bread and wine given for the purpose of
  remembering Jesus Christ and his sacrifice.

- Noncompliance with the Passover regulations for an
  Israelite meant that he would fall under the judgment of
  the community and be severely punished by being cut off
  from the people. Noncompliance with Jesus' directives for
  the Lord's Supper would cause the participant to miss an
  opportunity to be spiritually strengthened through reflection on the sacrifice of Jesus and consequently would
  lessen the likelihood of victoriously enduring the testing
  of one's faith.

- The significance of the Lord's Supper was actually much
  greater than that of the Passover, as surely as spiritual
  defeat is more significant than physical death. All the various sacrifices of the Old Testament were in some way
  looking back to God's plan that had been set in place
  before the creation, as well as looking forward to the
  realization of that plan in the person of Jesus Christ. Jesus
  was the ultimate sacrifice from which the very concept of
  animal sacrifice derived its meaning. He was "the Lamb
  of God who takes away the sin of the world!" (John 1:29).

Another widespread misconception is that the Lord's Supper works miraculously because of a priestly blessing pronounced over the bread and the wine. The custom of referring to the Lord's Supper as the "Eucharist" (a transliteration of the Greek word *eucharistia* meaning "giving of thanks") as early as the second century may have developed together with the idea that a designated cleric must preside over the Lord's Supper—since his blessing was also deemed essential to its proper celebration. In this scenario, the elements are somehow fundamentally changed and made holy. This view may have come about as the result of unconsciously connecting the observance of the Lord's Supper with the sacredness and holiness of the Old Testament sacrifices (as well as a literal interpretation of John 6 that will be discussed in the following section). As demonstrated by its first observance, the Lord's Supper did not inherently possess any sort of power to miraculously increase an individual's spirituality.

All the apostles physically shared in the bread and wine that were personally blessed by Jesus, but not one of them was prepared to share in his immediate suffering and death. For those who were present at the first Lord's Supper, subsequent celebrations would always serve as a reminder of their own weakness and lack of spirituality; Jesus had clearly warned them about the testing of their faith, but they had ignored his admonitions.

On the other hand, they would also be reminded of Jesus' humility and total dedication to the purposes of God. For Jesus, the Lord's Supper was an opportunity to graphically share with his apostles the essence of his purpose on earth and the depth of his love for both God and men. The effect of participating in the Lord's Supper was directly related to the condition of the individual's heart.

Finally, some would hold that the Lord's Supper is rendered ineffective for everyone involved if one of the participants is unspiritual or rebellious toward God's purposes (for example, having unconfessed sin in his or her heart). This belief may be reflective of the Old Testament teaching that every member of the congregation was to be ceremonially clean before participating in the Passover (Numbers 9:6). Some Christian groups have taken this idea so seriously that they require specific confession to be made before celebrating the Lord's Supper. Using the first celebration as a test case definitely relaxes such a legalistic requirement, since Jesus allowed Judas Iscariot to share in the Lord's Supper with the other disciples—despite his full knowledge of Judas' true spiritual condition.

Although some of these misconceptions may seem harmless enough, they are potentially false doctrines that can damage both the faith and unity of believers. Satan is determined to attack our understanding of the Lord's Supper, since anything with such power to unify the church and remind us of the sacrifice of Jesus can influence the effectiveness and productivity of every disciple. The rich detail supplied by the Gospel writers surrounding this first observance of the Lord's Supper works as an incredible safeguard against misinterpretation and false teaching.

The Bread of Life

The Gospel of John has no account of the Lord's Supper, but some have found in Jesus' words in John 6:25–70 a teaching that prefigured it. This deserves to be examined. Similarities are seen in the way that Jesus used "bread" in both instances to illustrate something about his nature and purpose, and also that he specifically asked his disciples to eat this bread. In addition, the miracle of feeding the five thousand (John 6:1–15) directly precedes this discourse and records that Jesus took the five loaves, gave thanks and distributed them. Matthew, Mark and Luke add that he "broke" the loaves as well—gestures that were all repeated in the Lord's Supper.

There are, on the other hand, some noteworthy differences. The imagery of the Lord's Supper draws heavily from the old covenant's sacrificial system, but the typology[2] of John 6 has to do with God sending bread—specifically, *manna*—from heaven to feed the Israelites in the desert. What is more, the significance of the "bread" is different in these instances. In the context of the Lord's Supper, the bread was meant to be commemorative, an aid to looking back at the one-time bodily sacrifice of Jesus. In John 6, the idea emphasized by the bread was *immediacy;* the presence of Jesus on earth gave spiritual sustenance then and there, beginning at the moment of acceptance and continuing for all eternity.

Some commentators have deemed John 6 to be a direct foreshadowing of the Lord's Supper, understanding that a literal interpretation of John 6 and its direct connection to the Lord's Supper supports the idea of "transubstantiation." This doctrine teaches that the bread and wine are miraculously transformed into the actual, physical flesh and blood of Jesus during the celebration of the Lord's Supper. However, there are many difficulties with this interpretation due to the language used by John:

1) *The words:* Many scholars agree that John's Gospel was written later than the other three Gospels and 1 Corinthians, which also has an account of the Lord's Supper. If this is the case, these earlier accounts of the Lord's Supper established the usage of the words "body" and "blood." If John wanted to demonstrate a direct connection between the passage in John 6 and the Lord's Supper, he likely would have used the same terms. However, John's use of "flesh" (never "body") and "blood" demonstrates that it was not his purpose to make a clear connection to the established accounts of the Lord's Supper. These accounts also used "bread" and "fruit of the vine"; but in John 6, Jesus spoke of "food" and "drink." Although the ideas are parallel, it is by no means obvious that John was referring to the Lord's Supper.

2) *The imagery:* In John 6, Jesus develops a theme. Beginning with the idea that the Son of Man has food to give men "that endures to eternal life" (v27), he reaches a crescendo in his final conclusion: "My flesh is real food and my blood is real drink" (v55). Jesus was making the point that as physical bread gives sustenance, so assimilation of his life and teaching can give sustenance to all men. On the other hand, Jesus used the bread of the

Lord's Supper to help his disciples reflect specifically on the meaning of his sacrificial death. The emphasis was on fellowship and participation in his sacrifice, as opposed to eating for spiritual sustenance. The ideas are similar but differ significantly in their emphases.

Throughout the Gospel of John, Jesus used figurative speech for stating spiritual truths, and his unbelieving listeners continually misinterpreted him. He told the Jews that he would destroy the temple—denoting his body—but the Jews thought he meant Herod's temple (John 2:18–22). He told Nicodemus that he must be born again—denoting baptism—but Nicodemus responded as if he thought he must somehow physically reenter his mother's womb (John 3:1–12). Jesus told the Samaritan woman that he had living water to give her—denoting the Spirit—but she understood him to mean some sort of physical water and questioned him as to how this was possible for him without a rope and bucket to retrieve it (John 4:4–24). John 6 simply continues this same pattern. Jesus told the Jews that he was the bread of God come down from heaven— emphasizing his life-giving purpose and teaching—but many of his listeners understood him to mean that they must literally eat his flesh and drink his blood.

This literal understanding of "eating his flesh" challenged many of Jesus' disciples to the point that they grumbled and even turned back from following him. Jesus asked them:

> "Does this offend you? What if you see the Son of Man ascend to where he was before! The Spirit gives life; the flesh counts for nothing. The words I have spoken to you are spirit and they are life." (John 6:61–63)

Unfortunately, to the unbelieving in heart, the meaning of these words was hidden. Jesus was not talking about his physical flesh. He was talking about that which was conveyed through his physical presence on earth: life and truth sent from God. When Jesus asked the Twelve if they also wanted to leave, Simon Peter answered,

"Lord, to whom shall we go? You have the words of eternal life. We believe and know that you are the Holy One of God." (John 6:68–69)

Peter's testimony confirms that he understood what Jesus was saying: his teaching was from God and the disciples needed to feed on his words.

Clearly there are parallels between the Bread of Life discourse and the meaning of the Lord's Supper. However, the conclusion that John 6 is a description of the Lord's Supper demonstrating "transubstantiation" is unreasonable. Although such a miracle would not be impossible for God to perform, there is no scriptural basis that warrants it. The Lord's Supper was meant to strengthen the disciples' resolve to follow Christ through contemplation of the sacrifice of his body and blood.

Washing the Disciples' Feet

The Gospel of John also provides the only account of another event that took place that evening: the washing of the disciples' feet.[3] As with the institution of the Lord's Supper, this deliberate act of Jesus was not part of the typical Passover celebration. It would be helpful to make a few observations about this particular instance of foot washing. Implementation of the normal Judean practice was obviously not Jesus' intention. Dinner was already being served and the usual custom dictated that the guests' feet were to be washed as they entered the house (see Luke 7:44). Also, Peter's vehement reaction to the thought of Jesus washing his feet demonstrates that this was the first time Jesus had ever attempted to do such a thing. It was in no way a common routine that he had practiced with his disciples. Therefore Jesus was using this custom to demonstrate a certain truth to his disciples: they still had not yet fully understood his heart and role as their Lord and Teacher.

Soon after having finished the Lord's Supper, the fellowship of the disciples digressed into an argument about which of them was the greatest. Jesus responded to their discussion by demonstrating his heart and humility through a down-to-earth act of service:

> He got up from the meal, took off his outer clothing, and
> wrapped a towel around his waist. After that, he poured
> water into a basin and began to wash his disciples' feet.
> (John 13:4–5)

Jesus explained his actions quite simply: "Now that I, your
Lord and Teacher, have washed your feet, you also should wash
one another's feet" (John 13:14). Jesus did not just want his disciples to compare themselves to him rather than to each other;
he wanted them to imitate his heart and attitude in dealing with
one another.

The purpose of this act was to demonstrate the humility necessary to be a true servant and to highlight the lack of such an
attitude among his disciples. At the same time, there are also
some interesting parallels between the action of having one's
feet washed and participation in the Lord's Supper. Ceremonial
cleanness was a vital issue when it came to participation in the
Passover celebration: those who were unclean were not
allowed to take part (Numbers 9:6). Although it is only reasonable to assume that all of the disciples were ceremonially clean
at the time of the Passover meal, Jesus indicates that there was a
whole other realm of cleanness and uncleanness—in the heart—
that should be considered.

Since Peter did not understand what Jesus was doing when the
Lord began to wash his feet, he protested. Jesus explained that

> "A person who has had a bath needs only to wash his feet;
> his whole body is clean. And you are clean, though not
> every one of you." For he knew who was going to betray
> him. (John 13:10–11)

If someone who has already had a bath goes outside and walks
around in sandals, only his or her feet need to be washed to
remove the dust and dirt that have accumulated on them in
order to be completely clean again. Participation in the Lord's
Supper was meant to have a similar cleansing effect: the casting
off of sin and guilt that so easily contaminate the purity (cleanness) of our hearts and consciences, as well as a refocusing of

our minds away from those worries and concerns of life that so easily distract us. Although Jesus told his disciples, "You are already clean because of the word I have spoken to you" (John 15:3), their behavior demonstrated that they needed a fresh reminder as to the significance of his life and coming sacrifice.

True disciples must be "born again" or "born of water and the Spirit" (John 3:3, 5) to begin their new relationship with God, a process that Paul referred to as "the washing of rebirth and renewal through the Holy Spirit" (Titus 3:5). Peter further explained:

> Baptism, which corresponds to this, now saves you, not as a removal of dirt from the body but as an appeal to God for a clear conscience, through the resurrection of Jesus Christ. (1 Peter 3:21 RSV)

Baptism is the spiritual washing whereby God removes the sin and guilt from our hearts through the blood of Jesus Christ. It marks the beginning of our new life in God's grace and supplies us with an unforgettable moment of conviction and joy. But Jesus understood how quickly we can forget our debt of gratitude and how easily we are distracted from good intentions and decisions.

Without taking anything away from the power of being baptized through faith to become sons of God (Galatians 3:26–27), Jesus instituted the Lord's Supper so that we would have a means to meditate on his sacrifice and be reminded of the cost of our salvation:

> For the grace of God that brings salvation has appeared to all men. It teaches us to say "No" to ungodliness and worldly passions, and to live self-controlled, upright and godly lives in this present age, while we wait for the blessed hope—the glorious appearing of our great God and Savior, Jesus Christ, who gave himself for us to redeem us from all wickedness and to purify for himself a people that are his very own, eager to do what is good. (Titus 2:11–14)

> Since we have these promises, dear friends, let us purify
> ourselves from everything that contaminates body and
> spirit, perfecting holiness out of reverence for God. (2 Corin-
> thians 7:1)

Refocusing on the heart and sacrifice of Jesus as we celebrate the Lord's Supper revitalizes and deepens our resolve to
live like Jesus. Gratitude is one of the most powerful motiva-
tions known to man, and as we reflect on Christ's incredible
sacrifice, we are powerfully motivated to live more wholeheart-
edly as disciples of Jesus Christ day to day. Just as a person who
has already had a bath needs only to wash his feet (John 13:10),
disciples of Jesus need to have moments of reflection where
they can refocus on the sacrifice of Jesus Christ. The Lord's
Supper uniquely provides us with such an opportunity.

Summary

There is no indication in the Gospels that Jesus was trying to
reinforce the keeping of the Passover or to carry over any of its
many regulations into the observance of the Lord's Supper.
Jesus devoted his final evening to fellowship, teaching and
warning his disciples of the imminent testing of their faith, and
in a very succinct way, the Lord's Supper captured the essence
of this message.

The abundant detail we have about the first Lord's Supper
allows us to analyze its effect on those who shared in it. The fact
that it did not have the same effect on everyone demonstrates
the importance of the attitude and faith of the individual. Even
when Jesus himself blessed the bread and the cup, it is clear
from the disciples' reaction that nothing mystical or magical
took place. Their hearts were not automatically made more
"spiritual" or "holy" before God. Further, Jesus allowed Judas to
participate in the Lord's Supper without protest, and his deceit
and hardness of heart did not invalidate the experience for the
others or desecrate the event. Each person was changed by
participation in the Lord's Supper to the extent that he allowed
himself to focus on God's will and the exemplary way in which

Jesus demonstrated the heart of sacrifice and obedience that each disciple must possess.

Many misunderstandings that surround the Lord's Supper seem to stem from conscious and unconscious associations made with the Passover celebration. Reviewing the details given in the Gospels confirms that neither Jesus nor the Gospel writers attempted to make such a connection. Although a group of people celebrates the Lord's Supper together, its effects are felt on a personal level and are dependent upon the thoughts and attitudes of each individual. And while the Law states that an Israelite who did not properly follow the Passover regulations—especially requirements having to do with ceremonial cleanness—was to be cut off from the people, we see no such penalty with regard to participation in the Lord's Supper. Though Jesus was fully aware of the spiritual condition of each participant before he broke the bread and passed the cup, he still allowed them all to share in the Supper with him.

Historically, there has been some confusion about the relationship between the Lord's Supper and Jesus' teaching that he was the "Bread of Life" in John 6. In both cases "bread" is used to symbolize an aspect of Jesus' purpose here on earth, and the eating of this bread is used to demonstrate an individual's acceptance of these purposes. But to interpret the bread of John 6 as an allusion to the Lord's Supper violates the word usage and imagery of the passage. The real danger in this type of interpretation becomes clear when the details of John 6 are pressed into doctrinal statements concerning the nature of the Lord's Supper and used to introduce foreign concepts like transubstantiation. It might be argued that, at a deeper level, the two ideas are identical—after all, fellowship with Jesus does give us spiritual sustenance. However, the meaning of the Lord's Supper and the meaning of the bread from heaven discourse cannot be considered synonymous, given that they draw upon very different Old Testament typologies. The language of the Lord's Supper has its roots in Old Testament-style sacrifice. In John 6, however, Jesus is specifically claiming to be the antitype of the manna that gave sustenance to the people of Israel in the desert.

That Jesus chose this particular evening to wash his disciples' feet for the first time suggests a possible parallel between that well-known custom and participation in the Lord's Supper. Just as a person who has already had a bath needs only to have his or her feet washed to be refreshed and feel totally clean, baptized disciples of Christ need periodic moments of reflection to remind them of Christ's sacrifice and of their commitment to imitate the heart of Jesus. Baptism washes away our sins by uniting us with Christ in his death and resurrection; focused participation in the Lord's Supper helps remove the distractions of temptation, sin and guilt (the dust of the world) and refreshes our hearts by reminding us of Christ's perseverance and sacrifice. As we remember how Jesus offered his body and blood, we are strengthened in our resolve to persevere whenever our faith is tested. Although there is nothing inherently miraculous in the celebration of the Lord's Supper, sharing in it can have the same effect that personally witnessing the miracles of Jesus once did: our faith is strengthened (John 20:31) and we are reminded of Jesus' power to forgive sins (Mark 2:10).

Notes

1. The fact that there is no specific mention of a "sacrificial lamb" or its consumption suggests an unproven but interesting thought—did Jesus present himself as the physical substitute for the lamb, and was the Lord's Supper an explanation of that substitution?

2. Typology involves the use of *types* that foreshadow and find their fulfillment in corresponding *antitypes*. "A type may be defined as an exceptional Old Testament reality which was specially ordained by God to prefigure a New Testament redemptive truth....Those who seek to interpret types must always remember:

- to give proper attention to the historical reality, noting especially its symbolic and redemptive significance to Old Testament believers and its subsequent continuation, commemoration, and influence on future generations of Israelites until its fulfillment in the antitype;
- to locate the chief point(s) of resemblance between the type and its antitype, and not to press the interpretation beyond these points;
- to relate the understanding of the typical significance to New Testament believers, not to Old Testament believers; and
- to interpret in the light of the established doctrines of Scripture rather than attempting to establish a doctrine on a type."

Source: John F. Walvoord, and Roy B. Zuck, *The Bible Knowledge Commentary* (Wheaton, Illinois: Scripture Press Publications, Inc., 1985).

3. Trying to understand the reasons behind Jesus' washing of his disciples' feet has been a source of much debate and discussion through the centuries. Some have demanded the literal adoption of foot washing as part of the celebration of the Lord's Supper or even as the mandatory beginning of any gathering of believers. Others have used this event to prove the idea that some of the commands of the New Testament were relevant only to that particular time and place and were never intended for the imitation or use of future generations. In this view, foot washing was never meant by Jesus to be literally imitated—anymore than imitating his style of dress or first century customs of food preparation. Another possibility preferred by this writer is that there was simply a deeper spiritual meaning behind Jesus' act of servitude and humility and that it was this attitude of the heart he held out to be imitated by his disciples.

6

Devoted to the Breaking of Bread

As we have seen, there are relatively few instructions regarding the celebration of the Lord's Supper when compared to the many verses of the Law that define the Passover commemoration. Similarly, the instances in which the New Testament describes the actual observance of the Lord's Supper are even less numerous than the meager Old Testament record of Passover celebrations. Outside of the Gospels, the only specific mention of disciples sharing the bread and the cup together is found in 1 Corinthians. Also, in contrast to the explicit Old Testament teaching concerning the Passover—designated as an annual celebration for the people of Israel on a specific day of a specific month—the New Testament never gives any similar directives about where or how often the Lord's Supper should be celebrated; Jesus simply said, "Do this in remembrance of me" (Luke 22:19). Our understanding of the frequency and circumstances of the early church's remembrance of Jesus can only be inferred from details in 1 Corinthians and from the use of the phrase "to break bread." In fact, our only possibility of confirming any reference to the Lord's Supper in the book of Acts depends solely on the meaning of this somewhat ambiguous phrase.

Jesus and the Breaking of Bread

The Israelites normally baked their bread in the form of oblong or round cakes, as thick as one's thumb and as large as a plate or platter. It was common practice to break rather than cut these loaves.[1] As a result, the phrase "to break bread" became an idiom meaning "to eat a meal," without reference to any particular time of day or to the type of food involved.[2] Significantly, the Gospels never use this phrase in such a casual manner. Jesus was often invited to eat in the homes of Pharisees, tax collectors, personal friends and many others. On such occasions, a variety of Greek words are employed to describe the act of sharing a common meal, including: "eating" (two different words), "reclining (to eat)" and "dining."[3] Although the act of breaking bread was commonplace, the phrase seems to have been deliberately set apart by the Gospel writers, since they do not refer to a single meal in this way—there is never an instance in the Gospels where a group of people is described as "breaking bread" together. In addition, it was customary in first century Judea to open the main part of a common meal with a blessing. The head of the house would give thanks with a piece of bread in his hand, which he would then break and distribute to those sitting at the table with him.[4] Although this practice is confirmed by the Gospel writers, Jesus is the only individual whom they describe as blessing and breaking bread in this manner. Therefore, something about the way in which Jesus "broke bread" caused people to view this familiar custom in a new light and to make use of this common terminology in a new and specific way.

The Gospels mention Jesus breaking bread on four different occasions: the feeding of the five thousand (Matthew 14:19, Mark 6:41, Luke 9:16), the feeding of the four thousand (Matthew 15:36, Mark 8:6), the Lord's Supper (Matthew 26:26, Mark 14:22, Luke 22:19) and Jesus' revelation of himself to two disciples on the day of his resurrection (Luke 24:30, 35). Although the circumstances are quite different in each of these instances, Jesus is always described as breaking bread in precisely the same way: he "took" the bread, "gave thanks" or "blessed" it, then "broke" it and "gave" it to those present. The consistent manner in which Jesus does this suggests that a pattern was established in the minds of his disciples. In all these instances Jesus broke bread as the head of the house to begin the main part of the meal—including the meal that we commemorate as the Lord's Supper.

Later, on the day that Jesus rose from the dead, he appeared to two disciples on the road to Emmaus, and walked and talked with them as they journeyed. He shared with them from the Scriptures, but they did not realize who he was—until they stopped for the evening and he took bread, gave thanks, broke it and began to give it to them. Luke recounts the story:

> They [Cleopas and another believer] got up and returned at once to Jerusalem. There they found the Eleven and those with them, assembled together and saying, "It is true! The Lord has risen and has appeared to Simon." Then the two told what had happened on the way, and how Jesus was recognized by them *when he broke the bread.* (Luke 24:33–35, emphasis mine)

It would certainly seem that there was something distinctive in the way that Jesus broke bread that infused this common practice with special significance.

The Bible specifically records that Jesus offered thanks or a blessing before every instance that he broke bread.[5] This was not unusual since the devout Jews in the time of Jesus were in the habit of blessing their food at mealtimes,[6] though it should be noted that the Old Testament contains no directives or examples of offering such a blessing. With regard to eating meals, many Pharisees and Jews of Jesus' day seemed primarily concerned with the outward details of their religion, such as the ceremonial washing of hands and dishes (Mark 7:1–3) and Sabbath-day restrictions (Mark 2:23–24). Jesus, on the other hand, focused first and foremost on God, consistently inviting his Father's involvement on every occasion of breaking bread by offering thanks or a blessing. John's description of the place where Jesus fed the five thousand affirms that such prayers were a prominent part of Jesus' practice of breaking bread:

> Then some boats from Tiberias landed near the place where the people had eaten the bread after the Lord had given thanks. (John 6:23)

Although "breaking bread" must have been somewhat routine for the crowd, the prayers of Jesus were obviously more noteworthy in their statement of intimacy with God and intensity of faith.

For the Jews, the breaking of bread marked the commencement of the main course of a meal. But whenever Jesus is recorded as breaking bread, it also marked the commencement of an extraordinary event—either a miracle or a moment of spiritual insight. The Gospels record that after Jesus broke bread:

- A few simple loaves were miraculously multiplied to feed thousands of people.
- His disciples were given an opportunity to reflect on the sacrifice of his body.
- The fact of his resurrection was confirmed to dis-believing disciples.

While it is reasonable to assume that Jesus also broke bread mundanely according to the custom of the times, these are never the circumstances that the Gospels specifically describe. In the Gospels, the breaking of bread seems to consistently signal an event of some importance. It would appear that Jesus chose the widespread custom of "breaking bread," and through the repetition of his own unique formula—"taking" the bread, "giving thanks" or "blessing" it, then "breaking" it and "giving" it to his disciples—he endowed the action with a new and greater significance. Never again would his disciples break bread together without thinking of their Lord and how he had lived among them and shared with them the power of his relationship with the Father.

The Church and the Breaking of Bread

After Jesus was taken up into heaven, the faithful apostles returned to Jerusalem and awaited the promised outpouring of the Holy Spirit. A few days later, on the day of Pentecost, this promise was fulfilled. It was on this occasion that Peter preached the first gospel sermon. The response was incredible, as about three thousand people accepted his message, repented and were baptized, adding greatly to their number. A new era in human history began as the prophecy of the coming kingdom of God was fulfilled and the church of God began to grow and spread upon the earth. Luke describes the body life of the infant Jerusalem church with these words:

> They devoted themselves to the apostles' teaching and to the fellowship, to the breaking of bread and to prayer. Everyone was filled with awe, and many wonders and miraculous signs were done by the apostles. All the believers were together and had everything in common. Selling their possessions and goods, they gave to anyone as he had need. Every day they continued to meet together in the temple courts. They broke bread in their homes and ate together with glad and sincere hearts, praising God and enjoying the favor of all the people. And the Lord added to their number daily those who were being saved. (Acts 2:42–47)

For the new converts of the Jerusalem church, the breaking of bread was a vital part of their community life. Although it would be grammatically correct to interpret this phrase as "the sharing of a meal together," there are at least three reasons within this text alone that would argue against such an interpretation. The first is their devotion to the breaking of bread.[7] The fact that the church in Jerusalem was as devoted to the breaking of bread as they were to the apostles' teaching, to the fellowship and to prayer, demonstrates a powerful emphasis. This intensity is best explained as a logical response to Jesus' commandment to break bread in the observance of the Lord's Supper. Second, as demonstrated earlier, the Gospel writers reserve the phrase "breaking of bread" for very special applications connected to the supernatural work of Jesus. Since the writer of Acts was one of these Gospel writers, any change in the usage of this phrase would normally have been signaled by an appropriate warning or explanation to his reader(s). Finally, we are told in verse 46 that the people "broke bread in their homes and ate together [taking their meals together, NASB] with glad and sincere hearts." If the breaking of bread simply meant sharing a meal together, then the phrase that followed—"they ate together"—would have been unnecessary.

All points considered, there is no reason to assume that "breaking bread" was now to be understood by its more common definition of the sharing of a meal together. Although Jesus took bread, gave thanks or blessed it, broke it and then gave it to his disciples on a number of different occasions, it was only in the instance of the Lord's Supper that he commanded his disciples to imitate him. From that time on, it would appear that whenever the New Testament describes a group of people breaking bread together, a clear reference to the celebration of the Lord's Supper is intended.

Apart from the account of the Jerusalem church breaking bread together in their homes, the only other celebration of the Lord's Supper recorded in the book of Acts took place during Paul's brief stay in Troas.

> ...But we sailed from Philippi after the Feast of Unleavened Bread, and five days later joined the others at Troas, where we stayed seven days.
>
> On the first day of the week we came together to break bread. Paul spoke to the people and, because he intended to leave the next day, kept on talking until midnight. There were many lamps in the upstairs room where we were meeting. Seated in a window was a young man named Eutychus, who was sinking into a deep sleep as Paul talked on and on. When he was sound asleep, he fell to the ground from the third story and was picked up dead. Paul went down, threw himself on the young man and put his arms around him. "Don't be alarmed," he said. "He's alive!" Then he went upstairs again and broke bread and ate. After talking until daylight, he left. The people took the young man home alive and were greatly comforted. (Acts 20:6–12)

Again, the fact that the whole group of people came together to break bread (v7) would most naturally be understood as the celebration of the Lord's Supper. Although Paul used this assembly as an opportunity for extensive teaching (perhaps too extensive for at least one disciple), it is clearly stated that the disciples met together for the purpose of breaking bread. After an unexpected accident punctuated the evening's program—and was answered by an equally unexpected display of apostolic power—Luke emphasizes that they continued their meeting and Paul "went upstairs again and broke bread and ate" (v11). As in Acts 2:46 where they "broke bread in their homes and ate together," the fact that Paul is reported as "breaking bread" and "eating" probably implies that the disciples in Troas also shared a common meal together, with Paul possibly presiding as the head of the meal.

Another reference to the breaking of bread can be found in the story of Paul's shipwreck during his voyage to Rome. Off the island of Crete, Paul warned the centurion of impending disaster; but his advice was ignored, and consequently, the ship ran into a terrible storm. After everyone on board had gone without food for two weeks, an angel from God came to Paul and said that all would be well. The next day Paul publicly shared this good news with the crew and passengers.

> After he said this, he took some bread and gave thanks to God in front of them all. Then he broke it and began to eat. They were all encouraged and ate some food themselves. (Acts 27:35–36)

Although this breaking of bread was clearly not the Lord's Supper, Paul took bread, gave thanks, broke it and gave it to everyone after the pattern of the head of the household. As an apostle of Christ Jesus, Paul also broke bread after the pattern of Jesus and invited them to believe in the angel's hopeful message of salvation. In the face of the storm, they were all encouraged by Paul's example and faith, and every one of them was safely delivered from death.

The final mention of "breaking bread" in the New Testament occurs in 1 Corinthians 10:16:

> Is not the cup of thanksgiving for which we give thanks a participation in the blood of Christ? And is not the bread that we break a participation in the body of Christ?

This breaking of bread unmistakably refers to the Lord's Supper, but we will reserve comment on this verse until we have looked at it in context in chapter 8.

As in the Gospels, it is clear that the phrase "break bread" was not used in a casual manner throughout the remainder of the New Testament. Either an individual broke bread as a way to commence a common meal or a group of people broke bread together in celebration of the Lord's Supper. As was the case with Jesus in the Gospels, the breaking of bread always marked the commencement of an extraordinary event—whether a miracle or a moment of spiritual insight.

Summary

Although the breaking of bread was a well-known table custom in the time of Jesus and historically became synonymous with simply eating a meal, the Gospel writers never used this phrase in such a casual way. In keeping with the common practice of the head of the house, Jesus is recorded on numerous occasions as taking bread, giving thanks, breaking it and giving it to those present. In the Gospels, Jesus is the only individual mentioned as breaking bread. Each time he did this it signaled not only the commencement of a meal, but that something special was about to take place. It may have been Jesus' foreknowledge of the institution of the Lord's Supper that motivated him to follow the same pattern each time he broke bread.

Jesus broke bread on four separate occasions—for at least three different purposes—but only one instance is singled out to be imitated and repeated by his disciples (Luke 22:19–20). Only the fact that Jesus had personally commanded his disciples to break bread during the Lord's Supper can satisfactorily explain the devotion of the early church to this practice. To remember Jesus specifically in the way that he had personally instructed them would prove to be a precious custom not only for them, but for all true disciples of Jesus in every generation. Just as John the Baptist redefined the ceremonial washing of his day, giving "baptism" (immersion in water) an entirely new meaning, Jesus broke bread in such a way that he gave it a whole new significance for his disciples.

This new meaning for the breaking of bread is confirmed in the rest of the New Testament. The young church in Jerusalem was devoted to it; Paul met with the church in Troas specifically to share in it; and Paul wrote to the Corinthians about its significance as a participation in the body of Christ.

Notes

1. *Enhanced Strong's Lexicon* (Oak Harbor, WA: Logos Research Systems, Inc., 1995), s.v. *"artos"* [bread].

2. Johannes P. Louw and Eugene A. Nida, *Greek-English Lexicon of the New Testament Based on Semantic Domains* (New York: United Bible Societies, 1988, 1989), s.v. *"aristaō"* [to have a meal].

3. Examples of these different words in context are: *bibroskō,* "to eat" (John 6:13), *esthiō,* "to eat" (Luke 7:36), *sunanakeimai,* "to recline (to eat) with" (Matthew 9:10) and *aristaō,* "to dine" (Luke 11:37).

4. Gerhard Kittel and Gerhard Friedrich, *The Theological Dictionary of the New Testament,* (Grand Rapids: Eerdmans, 2000), s.v. *"eulogeō"* [to bless].

5. The Gospel accounts use the verbs "offer thanks" and "bless" interchangeably on these occasions. The words are also used interchangeably in the New Testament to describe the thanks or blessing said over the bread and wine of the Lord's Supper: *thanks for the bread* (Luke 22:19, 1 Corinthians 11:24), *thanks for the cup* (Matthew 26:27, Mark 14:23, Luke 22:20 [implied]), *blessing over the bread* (Matthew 26:26, Mark 14:22) and *blessing over the cup* (1 Corinthians 10:16).

6. Much instruction concerning the saying of grace before and after meals is found in the Mishnah. See the section on "Blessings and Prayers" (*Berakhot*) from the *First Division on Agriculture* in Jacob Neusner, *The Mishnah: A New Translation,* (New Haven & London: Yale University Press, 1988).

7. *Proskartereō* means "to attend to constantly."

7

As in All the Congregations
of the Saints

While we do not have any record of a specific command given to Christians to begin worshiping on Sundays, "the first day of the week" emerges in the narrative detail of the New Testament as a special day of assembly for the churches. As noted in chapter 6, Luke specifically records that after Paul and his companions stayed for a week in Troas, "on the first day of the week [they] came together to break bread" (Acts 20:7). Having been in Troas for a full week, Paul could have chosen whichever day he wanted to call the church together; the implication is that an established pattern was already being followed, and to meet with the church meant waiting until they came together on the first day of the week. Although this is the only reference in the book of Acts to the first day of the week, Paul had already referred to it a few years earlier in his letter to the Corinthians, written during his second stay in Ephesus (see Acts 19):

> Now about the collection for God's people: Do what I told the Galatian churches to do. On the first day of every week, each one of you should set aside a sum of money in keeping with his income, saving it up, so that when I come no collections will have to be made. (1 Corinthians 16:1–2)

That there would be no need for a spontaneous collection upon Paul's arrival assumed that the Corinthian church was already meeting regularly on the first day of the week—just as the Galatian churches were also doing and probably the church in Ephesus as well.

One of the recurring themes in 1 Corinthians (one of Paul's earliest letters, written about AD 54) is a plea for unity. This plea was not just intended to unify the local Corinthian congregation, but to bring them into conformity with other congregations throughout the world. The following quotations bear witness to Paul's conviction about universal principles and practices that were to be shared by all the churches:

- Which agrees with what I teach everywhere in every church... (4:17)
- This is the rule I lay down in all the churches... (7:17)
- We have no other practice—nor do the churches of God... (11:16)
- As in all the congregations of the saints... (14:33)
- Do what I told the Galatian churches to do... (16:1)

These statements demonstrate that even before the apostles' teaching began to take written form as the New Testament Scriptures, clear principles were being taught and definitive practices had already been formulated in the church.

The First Day of the Week

The idea of meeting on the first day of the week to break bread appears in the Acts narrative without any sort of specific explanation (Acts 20:7). It seems natural to assume, then, that this custom had its origins in the earliest practices of the church and was universally understood and observed. Considering the fact that the early disciples often met with one another daily (Acts 2:46, 5:42, 19:9), it may have been the celebration of the Lord's Supper on the first day that distinguished it as special when compared to gatherings that took place on other days of the week.

The first day of the week possessed a special significance for the early church. First, Jesus prophesied that he would be raised from the dead on the third day following his death.[1] As every Gospel confirms, this turned out to be the first day of the week— our Sunday.[2] Second, Jesus waited a full week to appear for the second time to fellowship with his disciples, on the subsequent first day of the week (John 20:26). This interval seems to be deliberate and likely reinforced the special significance of the first day of the week in the minds of his disciples. It should also be noted that the Sadducees traditionally counted fifty days from the regular Sabbath (Saturday) of Passover week, so that for them Pentecost would always fall on a Sunday. It is likely, then, that the birth of the church also took place on the first day of the week.[3] Finally, it appears that the first day of the week was given a special designation by the time that John wrote Revelation, which begins with John's description of how he was in the Spirit on "the Lord's Day" (Revelation 1:10)—the day Jesus rose from the dead. The logic of this designation is further seen when one considers that the memorial act instituted by Jesus was already widely known as "the Lord's Supper" and was also being regularly celebrated on that day.

The Passing of the Sabbath

Although the New Testament writers gave the first day of the week special attention and set it apart from the other days of the week, we have no indication whatsoever that it was to be considered the "Christian Sabbath," with similar restrictions and regulations. Since the church began on Jewish soil and the first converts were previous adherents to Judaism, Sabbath day observance had long been part of their weekly routine and tradition. The New Testament overwhelmingly verifies the Jewish observance of the Sabbath and their practice of weekly assemblies in the synagogues each Sabbath day—our Saturday.[4] James, the brother of Jesus and the leader of the Jerusalem church, made the statement, "For Moses has been preached in every city from the earliest times and is read in the synagogues on every Sabbath" (Acts 15:21). The widespread establishment of synagogues and their well-established routine of meeting together played an important role in the initial spread of the gospel throughout the cities of the Empire. Jesus regularly went to the synagogue on the Sabbath (Matthew 12:9; Mark 1:21, 3:1; Luke 4:16, 6:6, 13:10); Paul and his companions usually began their ministry in the synagogue on the Sabbath each time they arrived in a new city (Acts 13:14, 44; 17:1; 18:4). These assemblies allowed missionaries like Paul to enter unfamiliar, foreign cities and quickly find an audience "primed" for the gospel message—an audience made up of both Jews and God-fearing Gentiles. Paul's commitment to meeting on the Sabbath day was directly connected to fulfilling his mission of proclaiming the gospel to all nations, beginning with the Jews first (see Romans 1:16). In fact, every reference to the Sabbath in the Acts narrative has to do with the meetings of the synagogue, and the term is never used with reference to the independent meetings of disciples.

A significant segment of the early converts to Christianity were Jews who continued to adhere to ceremonial requirements of the Law of Moses (Acts 21:20). Although many continued to follow Jewish customs—such as attending local meetings of the synagogue—this temporary situation was probably due to their incomplete understanding of God's plan.[5] The only specific New Testament teaching about the Sabbath delivered after the day of Pentecost appears in Paul's letter to the Colossians:

> When you were dead in your sins and in the uncircumcision of your sinful nature, God made you alive with Christ. He forgave us all our sins, having canceled the written code, with its regulations, that was against us and that stood opposed to us; he took it away, nailing it to the cross. And having disarmed the powers and authorities, he made a public spectacle of them, triumphing over them by the cross. Therefore do not let anyone judge you by what you eat or drink, or with regard to a religious festival, a New Moon celebration or a Sabbath day. These are a shadow of the things that were to come; the reality, however, is found in Christ. (Colossians 2:13–17)

Distinctions between ceremonially clean and unclean foods, as well as regulations to observe religious days, form part of the written code that was cancelled and nailed to the cross. Paul covers the complete spectrum of annual, monthly and weekly holy days in the Mosaic calendar when he refers to "a religious festival, a New Moon celebration or a Sabbath day." As the Hebrew writer so succinctly explains, "By calling this covenant 'new,' he has made the first one obsolete; and what is obsolete and aging will soon disappear" (Hebrews 8:13). Keeping the Sabbath day was a commandment that clearly belonged to the old covenant. As Jewish disciples grew in their understanding of God's plan for the church, more and more of them turned away from Moses. They even stopped circumcising their children and living according to Jewish customs—the very accusation brought against the ministry of Paul (Acts 21:21).

Breaking Bread in Their Homes

The New Testament seems to classify the gatherings of disciples into two categories based on their setting—public and in the home. From the very beginning of the church in Jerusalem, the private homes of disciples became centers of worship and fellowship. In fact, even before the day of Pentecost, the apostles were meeting together to pray in an upper room where they were staying, along with some women and the brothers of Jesus (Acts 1:13, 14). While the temple courts and synagogues proved to be vital aids for the spread of the gospel and the strengthening of the disciples in the period immediately following Pentecost, the early church was also in the habit of meeting in more intimate and familial settings:

> They broke bread in their homes and ate together with glad and sincere hearts, praising God and enjoying the favor of all the people. (Acts 2:46–47)

As we saw in chapter 6, the phrase "broke bread" is most logically understood to be the celebration of the Lord's Supper. The disciples' homes were probably the only venues that afforded the necessary freedom and privacy to celebrate this new custom in Jerusalem. It is exciting to imagine thousands of disciples meeting together in their homes throughout the city of

Jerusalem—and the effect felt in various neighborhoods because of the vibrant community life of this new movement.

Meeting in the temple courts proved very effective for hearing the apostles' teaching, enjoying the fellowship and joining together in prayer; however, meetings in the homes of disciples increased the opportunity and effectiveness of these activities even more. When Herod threw Peter into prison, we read that the church was earnestly praying for him (Acts 12:5). And where were they meeting? After an angel miraculously released him in the middle of the night, Peter went to the house of Mary, the mother of John Mark; it was there that many disciples were gathered and praying behind locked doors (Acts 12:12). And just as Peter knew where to go to find disciples meeting together in their homes, Saul also used this knowledge to go "house to house" when he was persecuting the church (Acts 8:3).

In Acts 5:42 we read that not only did the apostles preach and teach daily in the temple courts, but they also preached and taught daily "from house to house." More than twenty years later, Paul described his three-year ministry to the Ephesian church in very similar terms:

> You know that I have not hesitated to preach anything that would be helpful to you but have taught you publicly and from house to house. (Acts 20:20)

Some of these home visits may well have been to services of "house churches." We have already noted that the disciples in Jerusalem met together in certain homes, and Paul speaks specifically of churches meeting in the homes of individuals in Rome, Ephesus, Colosse and Corinth. In the last chapter of his letter to the Romans, Paul greets many members of the congregation by household and with the use of such phrases as "the brothers with them" and "the saints with them." At the beginning of these salutations, he specifically greets Aquila and Priscilla, together with "the church that meets at their house" (Romans 16:3–5).

We also have specific examples of entire households becoming disciples in Caesarea, Philippi and Corinth, which must have presented real opportunities for meetings in the homes of disciples in those cities. In Corinth, after the Jews in the synagogue had become abusive, Paul left them and went next door to the house of Titius Justus, a worshiper of God. It is implied that in this new setting, Paul continued to teach any who wanted to learn more about the gospel (Acts 18:7). After meeting Apollos at the synagogue in Ephesus, Aquila and Priscilla took him aside ("invited him to their home," NIV) and there explained to him the way of God more adequately (Acts 18:26). On his final visit to Jerusalem, Paul and his companions had the opportunity to stop and visit with the disciples in Troas (Acts 20:6–12). The church in Troas met together in an upper room, which was either the top story of a house or a room built on the flat roof of a house, sometimes having its own outside staircase. It is unclear as to whether this was the private home of a disciple or simply a rented facility.

Years later, after Paul arrived in Rome under Roman military escort and was waiting for his appeal to Caesar to be heard, he was allowed to live by himself along with the soldier who was guarding him.

> For two whole years Paul stayed there in his own rented house and welcomed all who came to see him. Boldly and without hindrance he preached the kingdom of God and taught about the Lord Jesus Christ. (Acts 28:30, 31)

Thus the Acts narrative ends in Rome just as it had begun back in Jerusalem three decades earlier—with disciples meeting together in their homes. As the disciples spread the gospel from city to city throughout the world, these "house meetings" would have provided a convenient setting for the celebration of the Lord's Supper, just as the homes of disciples had done so during the early days of the church. But unlike the early days, as the church spread outside of Jerusalem, the constraints on the celebration of the Lord's Supper disappeared. The way was now open for the Lord's Supper to be celebrated publicly at much larger gatherings—outside of the home.

The Pattern of Worship

To better understand the setting in which the Lord's Supper was celebrated, it will help us to learn all we can about the different activities that took place during a typical gathering of the church in the first century. To do so, we will first turn our attention to the forms of worship that developed in the Jewish synagogue. Since the early church was able to operate within the boundaries of established Judaism for a significant period of time—with some Jewish Christians continuing to honor the customs of the temple and synagogue just as they had done before their conversion[6]—the influence of the synagogue pattern of assembly on the infant church should not be underestimated.[7]

It would appear from the New Testament that there were some fairly standard practices that made up a typical synagogue service. Although we are not given an in-depth outline of the exact order of events, different passages give us glimpses into what would have been typical of a regular meeting of the synagogue. The following activities mentioned:

- Reading of the Law and the Prophets (Acts 13:15)
- Reasoning from the Scriptures (Acts 17:3)
- Preaching (Acts 9:20)
- Teaching (Acts 18:25)
- Words of exhortation (Acts 13:15, KJV)
- Collection for benevolence (Matthew 6:2)
- Prayer (Matthew 6:5)
- Reading letters from established religious authorities (Acts 9:2)
- Public judgment and punishment (Matthew 10:17)

Although there may have been other components of these meetings for which we have no record, the activities mentioned would have provided a foundation on which to base the church's program for assembly. Significantly, nothing in this pattern would have been at cross-purposes with the gospel. For the early church, the norms of worship and meeting together in the synagogue would have been understood from the personal

experiences of Jewish disciples and of many God-fearing
Gentiles. As a result, not much further clarification would have
been needed for them to be adopted and adapted for the benefit of Christians.

It is not difficult to find examples of activities within the assemblies of the church that correspond to those found in the synagogue.
Consider the following parallels to "church specific" practices:

- Reading of the Law and the Prophets (1 Timothy 4:13)
- Reasoning (from the Scriptures) (Acts 19:9)
- Preaching (2 Timothy 4:2)
- Teaching (Acts 20:20)
- Words of exhortation (1 Timothy 4:13)
- Collection for benevolence (1 Corinthians 16:2)
- Prayer (1 Corinthians 14:13–17)
- Reading letters from established religious authorities
  (Colossians 4:16)
- Public judgment and punishment (1 Corinthians 5:4–5)

The ease of this comparison suggests the adoption of these
activities into the assemblies of the church from the synagogue
meetings. It also explains the silence regarding the origin of
these practices in the churches; their continuation needed little
in the way of additional explanation or reinforcement.

The ability to faithfully celebrate the Lord's Supper was not the
only benefit of meeting together privately in the homes of disciples.
These meetings supplied numerous other opportunities for the
strengthening and encouragement of the disciples, including:

1) The freedom for new prophecy, revelation, knowledge or
   words of instruction to be presented without contest or
   dispute from the unconverted Jews (1 Corinthians 14:26);
2) The singing of hymns, psalms and spiritual songs with
   unveiled Christian interpretations and viewpoints
   (Ephesians 5:19–20, Colossians 3:16–17);
3) The ability to publicly read from the growing collection
   of prophetic writings (i.e., letters and Gospels), and the

freedom to treat them on an equal footing with the other "Old Testament" Scriptures (2 Peter 3:15–16).

Although the framework of the Jewish faith initially provided some support to the fledgling church, the seed of this new faith was being nurtured in the home meetings of the disciples. It was there that full expression was given to their faith in the risen Lord.

When we consider the content of 1 Corinthians and Paul's numerous reminders that all the churches were practicing the same things, it is noteworthy that a number of the issues being addressed involved the orderliness of their meetings when the "whole church" came together:[8]

> So if the whole church comes together…everything should be done in a fitting and orderly way. (1 Corinthians 14:23, 40)

In this context the phrase "whole church" would seem to refer to the full number of disciples in a city, even though they may normally have met in smaller units such as house churches (e.g., Acts 5:11, 15:22). Although Paul is addressing a number of problems and the lack of spirituality of the Corinthian disciples, we also learn that their meetings—which included the celebration of the Lord's Supper—were not taking place in their homes (1 Corinthians 11:22, 34). Paul specifically addresses issues such as speaking in tongues, women speaking publicly, fellowship meals and observance of the Lord's Supper. These practices had never been a part of synagogue worship as far as we know, but they may have been normal occurrences in the meetings of the house churches. It follows then that these activities in particular would have needed specific direction and teaching when the whole church came together—some being permitted, some being excluded and some being allowed only under certain conditions in the public assemblies (1 Corinthians 11, 14). Anyone who has witnessed a small "church planting" develop into a large congregation is well aware of the changes that take place in the dynamics of the gatherings as the membership increases in number and diversity. Retaining the sanctity and focus of the

Lord's Supper would have also had its challenges as the assemblies grew in size and the churches attracted more and more new converts.

Summary

As we read through the New Testament narrative, it becomes clear that the church had formulated a number of distinctive practices long before the apostles' teaching took written form as the New Testament scriptures. Paul also stated in his letter of 1 Corinthians that he expected conformity among all the congregations of the saints. Although no record remains of a specific command given to Christians, significant among these practices was the gathering on the first day of the week to celebrate the Lord's Supper. This custom simply emerges in the narrative detail of the New Testament as an established pattern. Whereas the first day of the week was given no special consideration throughout the earthly ministry of Jesus, from the moment of his resurrection, the day began to receive special attention—every Gospel confirms that Jesus rose on the first day of the week. By the time that John wrote the book of Revelation, the first day of the week was being referred to as "the Lord's Day."

From the early days of the Jerusalem church, the disciples were in the habit of meeting together in their homes. Not only did these meetings allow for the apostles' teaching, fellowship and prayer to take place, but they also provided a solution to the need for privacy to celebrate the Lord's Supper undisturbed. Throughout the book of Acts, as well as in most of Paul's letters, the use of the disciples' homes as meeting places is constantly highlighted. Some of the groups that met in homes were specifically referred to as "churches," emphasizing the significance of these assemblies for the disciples.

The role of the synagogue assemblies in the Acts narrative needs to be properly understood. Association with the synagogue was not meant to impose the following of Jewish customs on the church any more than the rules of the Passover celebration were to be joined to the Lord's Supper. Paul's commitment to meeting in the synagogues on the Sabbath was always evangelistic in nature, being directly connected to fulfilling his mission of proclaiming the gospel to all nations, beginning with the Jews. Although the early church adopted a number of elements of the synagogue worship service into their own assemblies, the unique witness of the church was centered on the good news of Jesus Christ and required them to meet separately and to develop their own program of worship. The celebration of the Lord's Supper seems to have been initially confined to meetings in the homes of disciples. As the churches spread beyond the borders of Judea and escaped the restraints of Jewish culture and tradition, the Lord's Supper was free to be observed more publicly and in much larger assemblies. Such developments required wisdom and insight on the part of the church leadership so that the Lord's Supper would not lose any of its meaning or effect in these less intimate settings.

Notes

1. Jesus referred to the interval between his death and resurrection in three different ways (two figurative and one literal). He said he would:

- destroy the temple and rebuild it in three days (Matthew 26:61, 27:40; Mark 15:29; Luke 2:46; John 2:19–20);
- give the sign of Jonah—three days and three nights in the heart of the earth—(Matthew 12:40);
- be killed and rise from the dead on the third day (Matthew 16:21, 17:23, 20:19, 27:63–64; Mark 8:31, 9:31, 10:34; Luke 9:22, 18:33, 24:7).

2. Neither the Mosaic calendar, prevailing Jewish custom nor pre-resurrection narrative of the Gospels attached any particular significance to the first day of the week. In fact, throughout the whole New Testament, except for this development with the first day of the week, no day apart from the Sabbath is paid any special attention at all.

3. Not all scholars agree that this method of reckoning was used during the year that Acts 2 describes. "The Pharisees, however, took the *sabbath* of Leviticus 23:15 to mean the first day of the Passover, the 15th Nisan, and thus counted seven full weeks from the 16th Nisan, so that Pentecost would fall exactly on the 59th day after the 16th Nisan....Prior to AD 70 the Pharisaic view seems to have controlled the observance." Gerhard Kittel and Gerhard Friedrich, *The Theological Dictionary of the New Testament* (Grand Rapids: Eerdmans, 1964, 2000), s.v. "Pentecost".

4. Although Sabbath day observance dates back to the Law of Moses, it would appear that the synagogue came into existence sometime during the Babylonian exile or upon Ezra's return to Palestine, or alternatively during the "intertestamental" period under the Hasmoneans. The temple lay in ruins and a new kind of gathering was needed to meet the needs of the dispersed Jewish people. For many of the Jews of the first century, the two ideas had become virtually inseparable: attendance at the synagogue was simply considered part of their observance of the Sabbath day.

5. Sabbath observance was not a requirement for the Gentiles, as was made clear in the letter sent out from Jerusalem after the conference in Acts 15 (about AD 49).

6. Paul testified that before his conversion, he went from synagogue to synagogue in Judea, Damascus and other foreign cities, fully expecting to find disciples of Jesus Christ in them whom he would take as prisoners (Acts 9:1–2; 22:4–5, 19–20; 26:9–12).

7. After Paul became a disciple, he imitated the ministry of Jesus by making it his practice to begin his missionary work in the synagogues of each new city he visited (i.e., Damascus, Salamis, Pisidian Antioch, Iconium, Thessalonica, Berea, Athens, Corinth, Ephesus, etc.).

8. In Romans 16:23, Paul was writing from Corinth and sent greetings from Gaius, "whose hospitality I and the whole church enjoy." This may mean that Gaius provided a facility where the whole church was able to meet—possibly even the venue in question here.

8

Participation in the Body and the Blood of Christ

I n 1 Corinthians 7:1 Paul writes, "Now for the matters you wrote about...," demonstrating that one of the primary reasons for writing was to respond to a letter that he had recently received from them. Paul spends the first six chapters of his letter discussing the attitudes necessary for unity among the Corinthian disciples and only then begins to address some of the issues they had written to him about. Although we do not possess a copy of that original letter from the Corinthians, we can infer from Paul's answers that at least six different questions had been directed to him. It would appear that every time Paul began to answer a new question, he marked this new section with the phrase, "Now about...." These section markers divide the remaining ten chapters of 1 Corinthians as follows:

- obligations of married disciples (7:1–24)
- obligations of unmarried disciples (7:25–40)
- food sacrificed to idols (8:1–11:1)
- spiritual things, traditionally translated "spiritual gifts" (12:1–14:40)
- the collection for God's people (16:1–11)
- the coming of Apollos to Corinth (16:12)

Although the Spirit allowed Paul to occasionally digress and teach on other subjects as well, a great deal of 1 Corinthians was spent answering the specific issues raised in their letter.

1 Corinthians is the only letter in the New Testament that mentions the Lord's Supper, and it contains two separate passages

that teach specifically on the subject. The first reference (1 Corinthians 10:14–21) occurs in a discussion about food sacrificed to idols and is significant because it introduces a new metaphor for the church: the "body of Christ." The second passage (1 Corinthians 11:17–34) is both corrective and instructional, possibly brought to mind by Paul's earlier mention of the Lord's Supper, and will be discussed in the next chapter.

Food Offered to Idols

Paul's reference to the Lord's Supper in 1 Corinthians 10:14–21 appears in his answer to the probable question, "Can a disciple of Jesus eat food offered to an idol?" His full answer to this question is found in 1 Corinthians 8–10. I encourage you to read these chapters and then the following summary of their contents.

Summary of 1 Corinthians 8
Almost all meat available in a city like Corinth would have made its way to the marketplace via the pagan temples where it would have been ceremonially offered to an idol. Some of the Corinthian disciples would have known that such ceremonies did nothing to change the fact that meat is a gift of God. After all, those so-called "gods" do not really even exist.

However, Paul warned the Corinthians to be careful with knowledge, since knowledge puffs up; it is love that builds up. Eating food offered to idols can be a stumbling block to the weak—they can defile their consciences by eating. If we misuse our freedom and eat in an idol's temple, someone with a weak conscience could be led into the sin of actually worshiping idols. In this way, our knowledge could destroy a weak brother, which would definitely be a sin against Christ. Be careful about how you use your freedom—it is better to give up eating meat altogether than to cause a brother to be idolatrous.

Summary of 1 Corinthians 9

Paul demonstrates by his own example that personal freedom must sometimes be sacrificed to allow the gospel to have its full effect. Although Paul had rights to be married and to receive support (as did any apostle), he did not demand those rights as a condition for his faithfulness or for having a serving attitude. He was even prepared to adapt and become like his hearers, so that in every way the gospel might be more effectively preached and received. Paul did not assume that since he preached the gospel he was some kind of exception to the authority of its message; he needed to submit to the gospel in the same way that everyone else did.

Summary of 1 Corinthians 10:1–13

When the Israelites escaped from Egypt, they thought that they knew God and how he wanted them to live. Their pride and confidence in their own understanding caused them to set their hearts on evil, and many of them ended up participating in idolatry. Most of them perished without receiving what was promised. Our pride in our own understanding can also deceive us and cause us to fall.

Summary of 1 Corinthians 10:14–33

Paul completes his answer by describing three settings where disciples could possibly come in contact with meat offered to idols: the idol temple (vv18–22), the market (therefore in the disciple's own home—vv25–26), or in the home of an unbeliever (vv27–30).

Although eating meat offered to idols means nothing in and of itself, Paul commanded the Corinthians to flee from idolatry. In the market or in the home of an unbeliever, they were to eat whatever was offered to them, the only exception being if they were aware that it could hurt another person's conscience. However, eating such meat at an idol's temple was to be totally avoided by disciples, since that would mean direct participation in pagan ritual sacrifice that could only be understood as an act of idolatry and rebellion toward God. We need to do everything to the glory of God, seeking the good of others rather than ourselves, so that many can be saved.

As we examine the details in this passage concerning the Lord's Supper, we need to remember that its purpose was not to lay a doctrinal foundation as much as to convince the Corinthians to avoid idolatry at all costs. The role that this text would later play in defining the Lord's Supper is demonstrated by the fact that it is the only passage in the New Testament where the word "communion" (KJV; "participation," NIV; "sharing," NASB)[1] is directly associated with the bread and the cup.

One Loaf Signifies One Body

> Therefore, my dear friends, flee from idolatry. I speak to sensible people; judge for yourselves what I say. Is not the cup of thanksgiving for which we give thanks a participation in the blood of Christ? And is not the bread that we break a participation in the body of Christ? (1 Corinthians 10:14–16)

Paul makes it very clear that food offered to idols means nothing at all. He wants to make sure, however, that the Corinthians understand that conscious participation in idol worship is still wrong. In his final argument, Paul seeks to demonstrate to the Corinthian disciples that they are already involved in a symbolic, sacrificial altar service: the Lord's Supper. The parallel between observing the Lord's Supper and pagan sacrifice is not readily apparent, since a contemplative memorial that consists of eating bread and drinking wine hardly compares to the drama of killing an animal and then eating and/or burning its flesh in pagan revelry.

To make this comparison more understandable, Paul describes the Lord's Supper from an unusual point of view: he chooses to emphasize our priestly activity in the Lord's Supper as opposed to our usual passive reception of the elements. In other words, rather than our customary eating of the bread and drinking from the cup, Paul stresses our direct imitation of the actions of Jesus—*breaking* the bread and *blessing* the cup. In the physical absence of Jesus, disciples now preside over the Lord's Supper and, like priests, participate in its preparation, blessing and distribution. This participation is more than just an imitation of action; it is a call to imitate the attitude of Christ, for it represents the sacrifice of his body and his blood. If the Lord's Supper is in fact an act of worship established by Jesus Christ, how can we make light of it by participating in a pagan ritual as well?

> Because there is one loaf [literally "bread," as in v16], we, who are many, are one body, for we all partake of the one loaf ["bread"]. (1 Corinthians 10:17)

The sacrifice of Jesus Christ is the one true sacrifice; all others are merely shadows of the truth (Old Testament sacrifices) or distortions of the truth (pagan sacrifices). And there is only one true celebration instituted to commemorate Jesus' sacrifice: the Lord's Supper. The church is built on this one sacrifice and committed to this one memorial. Not only do we have fellowship with Christ, but through this common participation, we have fellowship with one another as well. To participate in any other sacrifice would be to compromise and even dishonor the body of Christ—both his bodily sacrifice and the members of his church, his body.

It was pointed out in chapter 4 that *soma,* the Greek word for "body," developed a secondary sense during the fourth and third centuries BC: "a group of people." It is noteworthy that in this particular letter, where unity is one of the central themes, Paul chooses to introduce the concept of the church as the body of Christ.[2] By understanding that the body is a unit, made of many parts, and that we have all been baptized by one Spirit into one body (1 Corinthians 12:12–13), we are given a basis for unity that does not depend on individual strengths or personal decisions, but on the shared will of Jesus Christ in each disciple's life.

Participation in the Altar

> Consider the people of Israel: Do not those who eat the sacrifices participate in the altar? (1 Corinthians 10:18)

Sacrificial offerings were an integral part of the old covenant, and the Law of Moses included very specific instructions as to how each of these various sacrifices was to be offered. The purposes of these offerings were varied, and the regulations as to who could actually participate by eating of the sacrifice differed from offering to offering. Basically there were three degrees of participation by eating:

- *No one at all:* The burnt offering was not to be eaten by anyone at all—it was meant only for the Lord and therefore was to be totally consumed by fire. The person offering the sacrifice laid his hand on the animal's head so that it would be accepted on his behalf to make atonement for him. All sin offerings whose blood was brought into the Tent of Meeting to make atonement in the Holy Place were also to be totally consumed by fire and not eaten by anyone.
- *The person supplying the sacrifice:* Portions of the Passover lamb, the firstborn of the flocks and fellowship offerings (also called thank offerings and peace offerings) were to be eaten by those who offered the sacrifices, along with their households. This was an essential part of making these sacrifices acceptable to God.
- *The priest performing the sacrifice:* Portions of guilt offerings, sin offerings whose blood was not brought into the Tent of Meeting to make atonement in the Holy Place, grain offerings and offerings for priestly consecration were to be eaten only by the priests and their families. This food was for their sustenance and life. Certain parts of the fellowship offering were to be shared with the priests as well.

Participation in the altar and sacrifice was a concept that the people of Israel could understand on at least two different levels: the involvement of those who supplied the sacrifice and the involvement of the priests who prepared and killed the sacrifice.

As we celebrate the Lord's Supper, we need to contemplate the significance of Christ's sacrifice and its meaning for our lives. Through each of these different offerings, we can see a foreshadowing of the sacrifice of Jesus, as well as parallels to our participation in that sacrifice:

- Like the burnt offering, after men laid their hands on Jesus, he alone took their sins (and the sins of all men) upon himself (2 Corinthians 5:18–21).
- Jesus was the firstborn of God (John 3:16), the Passover lamb (1 Corinthians 5:7), our sin offering (Romans 8:3) and guilt offering (Hebrews 10:22).
- The blood of Jesus purchased men for God as an offering for priestly consecration (Revelation 5:9–10) and continues to give us fellowship with him and with one another (1 John 1:6–7).
- The grain offering made without yeast foreshadowed the bread that Jesus chose to represent his body in the Lord's Supper (Matthew 26:26).

All these sacrifices were in the Law to teach us about Christ, and Jesus completely fulfilled the requirements of each one of them (since he fulfilled the whole Law—Matthew 5:17, Luke 24:44) through his righteous life and atoning death on the cross. As we celebrate the Lord's Supper, we need to remember that our participation in Christ's sacrifice truly began at baptism when "all of us who were baptized into Christ Jesus were baptized into his death" (Romans 6:3). Only his sacrifice could make this participation possible.

Choose God, Not Demons

> Do I mean then that a sacrifice offered to an idol is anything, or that an idol is anything? No, but the sacrifices of pagans are offered to demons, not to God, and I do not want you to be participants with demons. (1 Corinthians 10:19–20)

Paul again repeats the facts: idols are not real, and food offered to them has no power. Nevertheless, God hates idolatry because at the center of this deception are demons that are seeking to corrupt the hearts of men.[3] A person involved in idolatry may become so deceived that he will never seek the true God. Understanding this peril, it would be completely wrong for a disciple of Jesus Christ to go along with the false (and powerless) rituals of idolatry—for his own sake and for the sake of his brother, who might see his actions and be completely deceived. Moses warned the Israelites about the influence of the pagan nations around them:

> "Be careful not to make a treaty with those who live in the land where you are going, or they will be a snare among you. Break down their altars, smash their sacred stones and cut down their Asherah poles. Do not worship any other god, for the LORD, whose name is Jealous, is a jealous God.
>
> "Be careful not to make a treaty with those who live in the land; for when they prostitute themselves to their gods and sacrifice to them, they will invite you and you will eat their sacrifices. And when you choose some of their daughters as wives for your sons and those daughters prostitute themselves to their gods, they will lead your sons to do the same." (Exodus 34:12–16)

The knowledge that idolatry itself is nothing can be dangerous if we do not realize that demonic powers stand behind it. Paul made a similar statement about the dangers of being naive to the apparently harmless traditions of men:

> The Spirit clearly says that in later times some will abandon the faith and follow deceiving spirits and things taught by demons....They forbid people to marry and order them to abstain from certain foods. (1 Timothy 4:1, 3)

Every disciple of Jesus needs to be on the alert against any teaching that might lead people away from the truth.

> You cannot drink the cup of the Lord and the cup of demons too; you cannot have a part in both the Lord's table and the

table of demons. Are we trying to arouse the Lord's jealousy? Are we stronger than he? (1 Corinthians 10:21–22)

A disciple cannot drink the cup of the Lord and have a part in the Lord's table if he is at the same time drinking the cup of demons and having a part in the table of demons.[4]

On the night that Jesus instituted the Lord's Supper, he said to his disciples:

"I tell you the truth, I will not drink again of the fruit of the vine until that day when I drink it anew in the kingdom of God." (Mark 14:25)

A little later that evening he also said:

"And I confer on you a kingdom, just as my Father conferred one on me, so that you may eat and drink at my table in my kingdom and sit on thrones, judging the twelve tribes of Israel." (Luke 22:29–30)

Jesus made it clear that in his kingdom he would drink the fruit of the vine anew with his disciples and share his table with them. At the time, the disciples did not realize that the inauguration of this new kingdom was just weeks away and that repeating the memorial meal that they had just celebrated would be the fulfillment of both of these prophecies. Each time we break the bread and give thanks for the cup, we have fellowship with Christ at his table in his kingdom. This incredible privilege of participating in Christ's priestly service and sacrifice should powerfully motivate us to distance ourselves from any action that could even hint at idolatry.

Summary

The structure of 1 Corinthians makes it clear that Paul was writing in reply to a letter he had recently received from the church in Corinth. The Corinthians had asked a number of questions, one of which was along the lines of, "Can a disciple eat food offered to an idol?" This must have been a troubling issue for the Corinthians since Paul devotes nearly three full chapters answering it:

- Although idols are powerless and the food offered to them remains simply food, enlightened disciples need to be considerate of their brothers and sisters who might be tempted to believe in the idols or their power (1 Corinthians 8).
- Paul uses himself as a real example of how mature disciples occasionally need to forfeit their rights for the benefit of others (1 Corinthians 9).
- He then uses the example of the newly freed Israelites to demonstrate how falling back into idolatry, immorality and discontentment can provoke God to anger, destroying the new spiritual beginning that he is trying to bring about in our lives (1 Corinthians 10:1–13).
- Finally, Paul discusses the different scenarios in which this sacrificial meat might be eaten. He basically says if it is from the market (eaten in one's own home) or in the home of another person and does not violate anyone's conscience, then go ahead—do all to the glory of God, seeking the good of others before yourself (1 Corinthians 10:14–33). Under no circumstances should a disciple blatantly participate in the altar of an idol temple. It is in this context that Paul draws a parallel with the Lord's Supper (vv14–22).

This teaching was not given as a basic description of the Lord's Supper, but was meant to emphasize the impropriety of disciples of Jesus involving themselves in idolatry.

Since we already break bread and bless the cup in our celebration of the Lord's Supper, how can we even think about participating in anything that remotely looks like the worship of idols? Paul demonstrates that the Lord's Supper was not meant simply to be a passive experience, but rather, an active participation in the priestly ministry of Jesus. The bread and the cup have profound meaning for disciples of Jesus, and this meaning would be diminished if we were also involved in the ceremonial eating of food sacrificed to idols. Besides, the one loaf that we share reminds us of our commitment to Christ's sacrifice and to his body, the church.

To help reinforce the charge that disciples should not be involved in pagan sacrificial rites, even though such rites are admittedly powerless and mean nothing, Paul introduces an interesting point about the Lord's Supper: it is a participation in what Jesus Christ accomplished at his own sacrificial altar. Throughout all history there is only one sacrifice that has been acceptable to God for the salvation of mankind; therefore there is only one loaf (one altar service and one sacrifice) that is pleasing to him as well. The Old Testament teaches that the average Israelite could eat a portion of three different sacrifices: the Passover lamb, the firstborn of the flock and the fellowship offering. The consumption of these sacrifices was part of their worship experience. In the case of guilt offerings, sin offerings, offerings for priestly consecration, and fellowship offerings, the priests and their families were allowed to eat certain portions for sustenance and life. The perfect sacrifice of Jesus completely fulfilled the Law and its requirements, including all these various offerings.

At the heart of the matter, the problem with idolatry is not in the food or in the images, but in the demons who stand behind such lies and deception. Jesus has prepared a cup for us to drink and a table where we can participate with him and with one another. It would be utterly wrong to defile that precious fellowship by association with demons and their deceitful schemes.

Most of us will never be offered meat that has been sacrificed to an idol, and few of us will be invited to eat a meal in a pagan temple. However, from the Corinthian experience, we need to learn that in the Lord's Supper we are having fellowship with the Christ who has offered the greatest sacrifice for us. We are deepening our unity with him and with his people. We are separating ourselves from all false approaches to God, and we are celebrating the fact that by the grace of God we have found him who is the way, the truth and the life.

Notes

1. This word "communion" (*koinonia*) and its derivatives have a range of meanings and applications in the New Testament. It is sometimes translated "fellowship" (Acts 2:42) and is well described a few verses later: "All the believers were together and had everything in common. Selling their possessions and goods, they gave to anyone as he had need" (Acts 2:44–45). It is also translated "gift" in the sense of a benevolent offering taken by one group to meet the needs of another group (Romans 15:26, 2 Corinthians 8:4). This idea carries with it the fellowship that results from sharing in the condition or situation of someone else—for the wealthy to share with the poor allows each to share in the other's condition.

2. The concept of the church being a body is mentioned only by Paul in the New Testament and was used by him to emphasize the unity that members of the church need to have in Christ. Paul was so emphatic about this teaching that he applied this term thirteen more times throughout the remainder of 1 Corinthians. In 1 Corinthians (about AD 54) and Romans (about AD 56), the concept was not yet fully developed and simply introduced the idea that the church was Christ's body with many members. Later, in the letters to the Colossians (about AD 60–62) and the Ephesians (about AD 62), the statement that "Christ is the head of the body" would be added to complete this picture.

3. "Sharing in divine power through common meals is an ancient idea which persists in the Greek concept of communion with the gods at sacrificial feasts or even by sexual union." Gerhard Kittel and Gerhard Friedrich, eds., *The Theological Dictionary of the New Testament: Abridged in One Volume* (Grand Rapids: Eerdmans, 1985), s.v. "koinonia."

4. Some have used this scripture to argue that no visitor at the celebration of the Lord's Supper should be allowed to participate. Since he does not belong to the body of Christ, it is maintained, he thereby somehow transforms the Lord's table into the table of the demons. There are at least two arguments I would offer against such an interpretation:

- Jesus had full knowledge of Judas' alliance with Satan and yet still allowed him to participate in the institution of his Supper.
- The nature of these tables is defined by their respective hosts, and not by those who are simply partakers at the table.

When people gather together in obedience to Jesus' request to remember him by means of the Lord's Supper, Jesus remains the presiding authority of the event since it is *his* table, the table that he instituted.

9

Examining the Heart

F or the Corinthian church there seemed to be some mis-understanding concerning the essentials of how to cele-brate the Lord's Supper. It would appear that the Corinthians (and quite possibly many other churches in the New Testament period) assumed that the Lord's Supper must always take place within the context of a fellowship meal.[1] It is not difficult to see why. As we have seen, the first instance of the Lord's Supper took place within the framework of an evening meal (the Passover celebration in the upper room), and it was subsequently the practice of the Jerusalem church to "break bread in their homes" (Acts 2:46). The bread of the Lord's Supper was never meant to appease the physical appetite, nor was the wine meant to lighten the heart or dull the senses. The purpose of the Lord's Supper is to remember the body and blood of Jesus and the incredible sacrifice of his life that was given for our sins. Of course, Paul sensed a much deeper problem in Corinth than just a misunderstanding about the proper form for the observance of the Lord's Supper in a public setting. The fact that any of the Corinthians could mistake their selfish, indulgent feasts with participation in the Lord's Supper demonstrates that they really did not grasp Jesus' intent or experience firsthand the power of contemplating the bread and the cup.

'No Praise'

In the following directives I have no praise for you, for your meetings do more harm than good. In the first place, I hear that when you come together as a church, there are divisions among you, and to some extent I believe it. No doubt

> there have to be differences among you to show which of
> you have God's approval. When you come together, it is not
> the Lord's Supper you eat, for as you eat, each of you goes
> ahead without waiting for anybody else. One remains hun-
> gry, another gets drunk. Don't you have homes to eat and
> drink in? Or do you despise the church of God and humili-
> ate those who have nothing? What shall I say to you? Shall
> I praise you for this? Certainly not! (1 Corinthians 11:17–22)

Something was definitely awry in the public assemblies of
the Corinthian church. The attitudes of the Corinthians were
arrogant and self-seeking, and their assemblies did little to
strengthen or unify the disciples. Paul's strong language makes
it clear that the worldliness of their meetings disturbed him
greatly. This same worldliness had manifested itself earlier
when Paul confronted them for allowing a blatantly adulterous
brother to remain active in the fellowship and for their pride in
the matter (1 Corinthians 5:1–13). This pride most likely did not
refer to inappropriate honor given to the sinful man, but to their
own ungodly tolerance of his sin. Worldly thinking often con-
fuses acceptance of the sinner with tolerance of sin.

Worldly divisions in the fellowship, rather than unity of the
body of Christ, characterized the meetings of the church in
Corinth. Some of the Corinthians were impatient, not waiting
for all the members to arrive; some satisfied themselves with
food, while leaving others hungry; and some even drank wine
in excess—to the point of drunkenness. And all this was done
in the guise of celebrating the Lord's Supper! The reason for
such disparity in the experiences of the Corinthian disciples was
probably due to their different social and economic situations.
Wealthier members would have been able to come earlier on
the first day of the week, while slaves—surely a good portion of
the church (1 Corinthians 1:26, 7:20–24)—and other poor members would have had to work all day before coming later. By the
time these poor members arrived, the rich had already eaten
and satisfied themselves. James also spoke out concerning discrimination against the poor in the assemblies:

> My brothers, as believers in our glorious Lord Jesus Christ, don't show favoritism. Suppose a man comes into your meeting wearing a gold ring and fine clothes, and a poor man in shabby clothes also comes in. If you show special attention to the man wearing fine clothes and say, "Here's a good seat for you," but say to the poor man, "You stand there" or "Sit on the floor by my feet," have you not discriminated among yourselves and become judges with evil thoughts?
>
> Listen, my dear brothers: Has not God chosen those who are poor in the eyes of the world to be rich in faith and to inherit the kingdom he promised those who love him? But you have insulted the poor. Is it not the rich who are exploiting you? Are they not the ones who are dragging you into court? Are they not the ones who are slandering the noble name of him to whom you belong?
>
> If you really keep the royal law found in Scripture, "Love your neighbor as yourself," you are doing right. But if you show favoritism, you sin and are convicted by the law as lawbreakers. (James 2:1–9)

Of all the places on earth where there should not be even a hint of favoritism or discrimination, the meetings of disciples should top the list. Worldly thinking elevates power, wealth and human talent, whereas God elevates the humble and those who seek him with all of their hearts: "Man looks at the outward appearance, but the Lord looks at the heart" (1 Samuel 16:7).

The example of Jesus teaches us that a man's worldly success does not necessarily reflect his spiritual condition before God. In fact,

> God chose the foolish things of the world to shame the wise; God chose the weak things of this world to shame the strong; he chose the lowly things of this world and despised things—and the things that are not—to nullify the things that are, so that no one can boast before him. (1 Corinthians 1:27–29)

If the one loaf of the Lord's Supper also signifies the one body of Christ of which we are all members (1 Corinthians 10:17), surely

Paul's conclusion was justified in view of the worldly and divisive thinking of the Corinthians: "When you come together, it is not the Lord's Supper you eat" (v20). By their attitudes and actions, the Corinthians were guilty of "despis[ing] the church of God" (v22).

Teaching from the Lord

These strong words of correction are followed by the only inspired account of the Lord's Supper outside the Gospels:

> For I received from the Lord what I also passed on to you: The Lord Jesus, on the night he was betrayed, took bread, and when he had given thanks, he broke it and said, "This is my body, which is for you; do this in remembrance of me." In the same way, after supper he took the cup, saying, "This cup is the new covenant in my blood; do this, whenever you drink it, in remembrance of me." (1 Corinthians 11:23–25)

Paul's emphasis affirms what has already become apparent from our discussion in chapter 5: Jesus intended neither a permanent association with the Passover celebration nor the need for an accompanying fellowship meal—these were circumstantial associations, not mandatory. Paul's account of the Lord's Supper is almost identical to Luke's, except that when Jesus presented the cup to his disciples, Paul records the words, "Do this, whenever you drink it, in remembrance of me." It is only the simple breaking of bread and the sharing of the cup that constitute the Lord's Supper proper, as instituted by Jesus. Paul's account also emphasizes the memorial nature of the Lord's Supper since, after both the bread and the cup, Jesus repeats the phrase: "Do this in remembrance of me." The Lord's Supper was never intended to provide physical sustenance, but to aid in remembering Jesus through the unadorned sharing of the bread and the cup— just as he asked us to do. This remembrance is the source of true spiritual sustenance.

When celebrated properly, the Lord's Supper is a testimonial of our personal faith in the death and sacrifice of Jesus Christ. It is therefore an opportunity to be strengthened by the expression of the faith of others around us:

> For whenever you eat this bread and drink this cup, you pro-
> claim the Lord's death until he comes. (1 Corinthians 11:26)

The physical death of Jesus emphasized both his human frailty and his obedience, and remembering these realities of Christ's physical nature helps each one of us to live our lives with the right heart and attitude. In addition, proclaiming his death "until he comes" reminds us of the reality of his resurrection and of his current reign in power that will be consummated at his return. Each time we observe the Lord's Supper, we repeat this proclamation of Christ's sacrifice and death until he comes. The word "whenever" (also found in v25) makes it clear that though we have no word of Jesus stating how often the Lord's Supper should be celebrated, he had a definite expectation that it would be done consistently and with the same meaning that he had given it. The Lord's Supper is meant to be a significant spiritual experience every time it is celebrated—never just a legalistic obligation.

A Worthy Manner

After repeating the simple directions as given by Jesus in the Gospel accounts, Paul goes on to give some of the most pro-found insight concerning the Lord's Supper found in the New Testament:

> Therefore, whoever eats the bread or drinks the cup of the
> Lord in an unworthy manner will be guilty of sinning against
> the body and blood of the Lord. (1 Corinthians 11:27)

The Lord's Supper needs to be taken worthily. The Greek word for "worthy," *axios*, literally means "bringing into balance."[2] This word is most simply understood as the direct relationship between an action and the payment that it deserves: "the laborer is worthy of his wages" (Luke 10:7, NASB). It is also used to describe actions that appropriately express a certain state of mind or status: "fruit in keeping with [worthy of] repen-tance" (Matthew 3:8), and even the right response to the undeserved opportunity of receiving God's grace: because they rejected the message, the Jews did "not consider [themselves] worthy of eternal life" (Acts 13:46). In the book of Revelation, John wept because no one was found "in heaven or on earth or under the earth" who was "worthy to open the scroll" (Revelation 5:3–4). Then he saw a Lamb looking as if it had been slain and heard the song:

> "You are worthy to take the scroll
>   and to open its seals,
> because you were slain,
>   and with your blood you purchased men for God
>   from every tribe and language and people and nation.
> You have made them to be a kingdom and priests to
>   serve our God,
>   and they will reign on the earth."

> In a loud voice they sang:

> "Worthy is the Lamb, who was slain,
>   to receive power and wealth and wisdom and strength
>   and honor and glory and praise!" (Revelation 5:9–10, 12)

Jesus was "worthy" because only his life and sacrifice could purchase our place in God's kingdom. As Peter so eloquently stated,

> "Salvation is found in no one else, for there is no other name
> under heaven given to men by which we must be saved."
> (Acts 4:12)

When we consider the full meaning of the sacrifice of the body and blood of Jesus Christ, God expects our hearts to respond in a worthy manner. As Jesus said, "Anyone who does not take his cross and follow me is not worthy of me" (Matthew 10:38). Remembering the sacrifice of Jesus motivates a true disciple to offer his or her own life with a Christlike attitude. After the first Lord's Supper, Jesus asked his disciples to consider his example of humility and service, and to imitate him by living the same way in relationship with each other (Luke 22:25–27). Either we demonstrate our acceptance of Christ's sacrifice by accepting the standard of his life and changing the way that we live, or we reject his sacrifice and receive no benefit from it—proving ourselves to be unworthy of it.

Examining Ourselves

> A man ought to examine himself before he eats of the bread and drinks of the cup. (1 Corinthians 11:28)

When we look back on the evening in which Jesus was betrayed, we read of Jesus repeatedly warning his disciples of the weakness of their flesh and the arrogance of their self-confidence. Jesus tried again and again to get the disciples to understand the condition of their hearts and just how unprepared they really were for the imminent testing of their faith. The disciples were amazingly quick to call Jesus "Lord" in one breath, only to argue and disagree with him in the next. The Corinthians seemed no less distracted from Christ's purposes than the original Twelve had been. They were focusing on superficial things, such as their physical appetites and judging each other by worldly standards—rather than on the state of their own hearts before God.

The idea of examining oneself is key to properly observing the Lord's Supper, and Paul gives us more insight into how to do this in some of his other letters:

> Examine yourselves to see whether you are in the faith; test yourselves. Do you not realize that Christ Jesus is in you—unless, of course, you fail the test? (2 Corinthians 13:5)

Disciples need to have a sober estimate of the quality of their faith and of the true effect of Christ indwelling them by his Spirit. The Christian experience is not simply a new system of rules for living, but a new spiritual *life* based on the transforming presence of Jesus in our hearts. If we cannot believe that Christ is in us, how can we believe that we are in Christ?

> If anyone thinks he is something when he is nothing, he deceives himself. Each one should test his own actions. Then he can take pride in himself, without comparing

> himself to somebody else, for each one should carry his
> own load. (Galatians 6:3–5)

It is so typical for us to compare ourselves to others in areas in which we are confident of our strengths, while ignoring our areas of weakness and sin. Instead, we need to be thankful for whatever we have received—since all good things are from above (James 1:17)—as well as for the opportunity to grow stronger through grace. Therefore, as we are transformed by knowing Christ, all the glory and praise is given to God.

The secret of examining oneself is to use Christ as the only true mirror, rejecting both our own standards and the standards of those around us. As we examine Christ in the Lord's Supper, we need to examine ourselves as well.

Eating and Drinking Judgment

> For anyone who eats and drinks without recognizing the
> body of the Lord eats and drinks judgment on himself.
> (1 Corinthians 11:29)

Eating or drinking without appreciating the meaning of the Lord's Supper brings judgment on the individual.[3] The message of both the bread and the cup are so obvious that our response to them truly defines the spiritual status of our hearts. This same principle was demonstrated by Jesus in the Parable of the Sower, in which a farmer did not prejudge the different kinds of soils that he encountered, but indiscriminately sowed his seed everywhere—a foolish farmer according to conventional wisdom (Mark 4:3–20). The true nature of each type of soil was shown by its response to what was sown, and therefore judgment as to the condition of each soil was not simply a matter of preliminary observation, but an issue of its ultimate fruitfulness. Of course, one obvious conclusion of this parable is that although God's word is sown in the hearts of men with the possibility of producing a harvest, the true nature of every heart will be exposed by each individual's response. Each time we participate in the Lord's Supper, we are faced with the message of Christ's death and sacrifice, and the condition of our own hearts will be shown by our resultant attitudes and decisions.

The fact that Jesus came to earth and became the perfect sacrifice for our sin is a double-edged sword. As Paul wrote:

> Therefore, there is now no condemnation for those who are in Christ Jesus, because through Christ Jesus the law of the Spirit of life set me free from the law of sin and death. For what the law was powerless to do in that it was weakened by the sinful nature, God did by sending his own Son in the likeness of sinful man to be a sin offering. And so he condemned sin in sinful man, in order that the righteous requirements of the law might be fully met in us, who do not live according to the sinful nature but according to the Spirit. (Romans 8:1–4)

This perfect sacrifice of Jesus not only gives salvation to those who are in Christ, but also completely condemns every person that has ever lived. Jesus shared in our physical nature, was tempted as we are and yet was without sin—so we have no excuse. Either we accept our responsibility for his death because it was our sin that put him on the cross, or we reject his offer of forgiveness and stand totally condemned without any possibility of salvation. Since one definition of judgment is "the process of forming an opinion or evaluation by discerning and comparing,"[4] observing the Lord's Supper can discern the condition of our hearts by comparing them to the heart of Christ. Just like when we are presented with God's word, participation in the Lord's Supper "judges the thoughts and attitudes of the heart" (Hebrews 4:12). Since eternal life is to know the Father and the Son (John 17:3), eating the bread or drinking the cup with ungratefulness or indifference condemns us by demonstrating the orientation of our hearts:

> That is why many among you are weak and sick, and a number of you have fallen asleep. (1 Corinthians 11:30)

According to the Gospel accounts, even the Twelve did not partake of the Lord's Supper worthily their first time, since their reflection upon the body and blood of Christ did not have any noticeable spiritual effect. Immediately after the disciples finished the Lord's Supper, a dispute arose among them as to which of them was the greatest (Luke 22:24). Their self-centered response should have served as a warning signal about just how spiritually unprepared they really were. Later that evening in Gethsemane, while Jesus was wrestling in prayer with the Father's will, he returned to where he had left the disciples and found them sleeping and said, "The spirit is willing, but the body is weak" (Matthew 26:41). Since the disciples were not even ready to "watch and pray" with Jesus, it is not surprising that, when faced with the challenge to stand and suffer with him at the moment of his arrest, they ran away to save their lives.

For many of the Corinthians, celebrating the Lord's Supper was as ineffective in strengthening them spiritually as it had been for the Twelve that first night. Many were weak and sick (spiritually powerless), and some had even fallen asleep.[5] If we focus on the sacrifice of Christ's body and blood as he has asked us to do, we will then be able to face the challenges of truly being Christ's disciples. Instead of being weak, powerless or falling asleep, we will be strong and alert, ready to go through any trial with faithfulness and perseverance.

There is also an added nuance to these verses because of the metaphor introduced in 1 Corinthians 10:17: "Because there is one loaf, we who are many, are one body, for we all partake of the one loaf." People who eat and drink the bread and the cup without recognizing the church and the spiritual needs of her members, judge themselves of not having a Christlike attitude. This lack of concern for each other's spiritual condition could be seen as contributing to the condition of many being weak, sick and even in some cases, asleep.

Judgment Without Condemnation

> But if we judged ourselves, we would not come under judgment. (1 Corinthians 11:31)

Judgment that comes voluntarily from within our own hearts brings a totally different result than judgment that must be imposed from the outside. Jesus aptly described this voluntary humbling of ourselves when he identified himself as the stone rejected by the builders but made into the cornerstone—

"Everyone who falls on that stone will be broken to pieces, but he on whom it falls will be crushed." (Luke 20:18)

The principle is simple and clear: either we willingly humble ourselves before Christ and accept his life as the standard for our lives, or we will be forcibly humbled and destroyed by God's judgment in the end. The Lord's Supper is a God-ordained moment of self-evaluation, instituted so that every faithful disciple of Jesus can stay on the right path and avoid a crushing final judgment.

For Paul this self-evaluation was in no way negative, but was in fact necessary to fulfill his greatest passion—the passion to know Christ more completely.

I want to know Christ and the power of his resurrection and the fellowship of sharing in his sufferings, becoming like him in his death, and so, somehow, to attain to the resurrection from the dead.

Not that I have already obtained all this, or have already been made perfect, but I press on to take hold of that for which Christ Jesus took hold of me. Brothers, I do not consider myself yet to have taken hold of it. But one thing I do: Forgetting what is behind and straining toward what is ahead, I press on toward the goal to win the prize for which God has called me heavenward in Christ Jesus.

All of us who are mature should take such a view of things. And if on some point you think differently, that too God will make clear to you. Only let us live up to what we have already attained. (Philippians 3:10–16)

It is this desire to know Christ that motivates us to continually reevaluate our spiritual condition. Conversion and baptism are just the beginning of our walk with God; it is in our day to day struggles that we are truly given the opportunity by God to know Christ's heart and the power of his resurrection. Like Paul, we need to forget what lies behind—whether success or victory—and strive toward the goal to win the prize for which God has called us heavenward. We have been called to share in his glory, but this is only possible if we share in his sufferings (Romans 8:17), for even Jesus learned obedience and was made perfect by what he suffered (Hebrews 5:8–9). Jesus is the author and perfecter of our faith, and only by following him will we go to be with the Father as he has promised.

> When we are judged by the Lord, we are being disciplined so that we will not be condemned with the world. (1 Corinthians 11:32)

For those who truly want to be Christ's disciples, a heart-level comparison of our lives to the standard of Jesus is not only a humbling exercise, but a true discipline from God. No matter how much we have tried to do or have already accomplished, the fact is that in comparison to Christ, we will always come up lacking. We can sometimes become discouraged because of our constant battle with weakness, temptation and sin and the resultant need to be constantly humble before the cross. Satan tempts us to think that if we cannot be perfect, there is no point in even trying. Although the Lord's Supper is a reminder of the consequence of our sin and imperfection, it should also help us to remember God's perfect love and plan for our lives.

Everyone sins, and sin is detestable to God, but there is a response that a sinner can have toward sin that even God considers worthy and right: godly sorrow.

> Godly sorrow brings repentance that leads to salvation and leaves no regret, but worldly sorrow brings death. See what this godly sorrow has produced in you: what earnestness, what eagerness to clear yourselves, what indignation, what alarm, what longing, what concern, what readiness to see justice done. At every point you have proved yourselves to be innocent in this matter. (2 Corinthians 7:10–11)

When someone sins, only two conditions of the heart are possible: either the person has acted according to his or her established moral principles and would act the same way again if presented with similar opportunity; or due to weakness, ignorance or a momentary lapse of self-control, the person has acted contrary to how he or she really wants to behave, and deep down in his or her heart, really wants to do the right thing (Romans 7:14–25). Godly sorrow that brings repentance is the only way that we can prove to God that our hearts are in the second condition—it proves us innocent of *wanting* to be sinners, but not innocent of having sinned. This godly sorrow will be clearly evidenced by our admission of guilt and a decision for personal change. It will also be clearly demonstrated by the energy we are willing to put into our Christian lives. If we judge ourselves properly, the result will always be godly sorrow for our sin, and the resulting repentance will bring a longing to see justice done and for righteousness to prevail. To take the Lord's Supper in a worthy manner, we must humbly accept God's righteous judgment of our sinful condition. At the same time, we need to fully repent of our sins, remembering that godly sorrow always leads to salvation.

Although Jesus clearly meant for the celebration of the Lord's Supper to be a serious focal point, it was never intended to be overwhelming or depressing. He wanted the remembrance of his body and blood to energize his disciples toward greater acts of love and obedience. Unfortunately, this result is only possible if the participant is softhearted and open to the message of the cross. For those who are hardhearted and stubborn, the Lord's Supper will have no other consequence but to condemn:

> "As for the person who hears my words but does not keep them, I do not judge him. For I did not come to judge the world, but to save it. There is a judge for the one who rejects me and does not accept my words; that very word which I spoke will condemn him at the last day. For I did not speak of my own accord, but the Father who sent me commanded me what to say and how to say it. I know that his

> command leads to eternal life. So whatever I say is just
> what the Father has told me to say." (John 12:47–50)

The Lord's Supper is a time for serious self-examination and also for deep reflection on the sacrifice and heart of Jesus. God's incredible offer of salvation through Jesus Christ can only be received of one's own free will. To reject God's offer is to reject salvation, and therefore to invite sure condemnation on the last day.

> So then, my brothers, when you come together to eat, wait
> for each other. If anyone is hungry, he should eat at home, so
> that when you meet together it may not result in judgment.
> And when I come I will give further directions. (1 Corinthians 11:33–34)

Paul's final admonitions were simple: observe the Lord's Supper correctly, both in form and in attitude. The Corinthians were to show concern for each other, and none were to view the Lord's Supper as a means of physical sustenance—those types of meals could be had at home. By meeting together properly, the Corinthians would avoid condemnation from God. And when Paul arrived on his next visit, he would give them further direction concerning these things, as found in 2 Corinthians.

Summary

At this time in their history, Paul was not at all pleased with the level of spirituality in the public assemblies of the Corinthian church. One of their specific problems was the manner in which they were celebrating the Lord's Supper. Instead of a Christ-centered moment of reflection and renewal, the Corinthians were having an indulgent feast, marred by selfishness and arrogance toward one another. Paul told them explicitly that such a meal was *not* the Lord's Supper, but the problem was much more than a technical one: the Corinthians seemed to have lost the whole focus of the celebration. Paul recounted to them the words of Jesus concerning the bread and the cup, and clearly showed them that Christ's purpose was simple: "Do this in remembrance of me."

The celebration of the Lord's Supper is to be a time of reflection on one's own spiritual condition and on the sacrifice of Jesus Christ. It is meant to be a moment of sober estimation of the level of one's faith, as well as a time when comparison with others and worldly standards are set aside. In the Lord's Supper, the life and sacrifice of Jesus need to be the mirror into which each disciple looks to see his or her true reflection, leading to greater humility, recommitment of his or her life and gratefulness to God for Christ's perfect sacrifice. Each time we celebrate the Lord's Supper, we are faced with a choice: to judge ourselves by using Jesus as our standard or to be condemned by God. God desires for us to voluntarily humble ourselves before him and to rededicate our lives to the imitation and glory of his Son. To make this judgment incorrectly will, at the very least, result in spiritual weakness, sickness and sleep—and in rare cases may even lead to God's condemnation through sickness and physical death. The bottom line is this: if we don't focus on Jesus and his sacrifice, there is no way that we will be victorious in the testing of our faith. Without this softening of our hearts and strengthening of our resolve, we will simply follow the desires of our flesh and fail the spiritual test every time.

The memory of Christ's love and sacrifice ought absolutely to be an encouraging and positive thought, but a sober estimate of our own spiritual condition can sometimes be disheartening. We must never forget that there is a response to our own sin that God considers worthy and right: godly sorrow. Although God's ultimate will is that we do not sin at all, in our weakness, God allows us to approach him worthily when we have acknowledged our sin and are determined not to consciously sin again—that is, when we repent. Above all other activities, the celebration of the Lord's Supper should have fortified the spirituality of the Corinthians. As it was, they had allowed their worldliness and divisiveness to taint the sharing of the bread and the cup, and their meetings were doing "more harm than good" (1 Corinthians 11:17). Although the Lord's Supper is to be celebrated as a group, the focus of each participant is to be on the significance of the sacrifice of Jesus for his or her own life. Worthiness needs to be characteristic of each participant's heart; and for this reason "a man ought to examine himself before he eats" (1 Corinthians 11:28).

Notes

1. By the time the last few letters of the New Testament were written, the fellowship meal seems to have acquired a name—the "love feast." Jude 12 and 2 Peter 2:13 describe the occasion of disciples gathering to "feast together" (Gr., *suneuōcheomai*) in the "love (feast)" (Gr., *agapē*). For the alternative view, namely, that we should consider having the Lord's Supper in the context of a fellowship meal today, see Douglas Jacoby's essay "Putting 'Supper' Back in the Lord's Supper" in his book *Q & A, Volume 2: More Answers to Bible Questions You Have Asked* (Billerica, Mass.: DPI, 2002), 186–202.

2. The Greek word for "worthy" (*axios*) literally means "bringing into balance." (Gerhard Kittel and Gerhard Friedrich, eds., *Theological Dictionary of the New Testament: Abridged in One Volume*, [Grand Rapids: Eerdmans, 1985], s.v. "axios.") This word is often used to speak of the direct relationship between an action and the payment that it deserves:

- worker worthy of his wages (Matthew 10:10, Luke 10:7, 1 Timothy 5:18)
- sinners worthy of punishment (Luke 12:48)
- benevolent centurion worthy of help (Luke 7:1–4)
- sinful son no longer worthy of a son's rights (Luke 15:19–21)
- crime worthy of death (Luke 23:15, 41; Acts 23:29, 25:11–25, 26:31; Romans 1:32)
- master worthy of a slave's respect (1 Timothy 6:1)
- God worthy of glory, honor and power since he created all things (Revelation 4:11)
- Jesus worthy to open the book (Revelation 5:2, 4, 9, 12)
- sinful earth worthy of being given blood to drink (Revelation 16:6)

Axios can also be used to describe actions appropriately expressing a certain state of mind or status:

- fruits worthy of repentance (Matthew 3:8, Luke 3:8, Acts 26:20)
- priorities that show one worthy of being a disciple (Matthew 10:37–38)
- worthy of untying Jesus' sandals (John 1:27, Acts 13:25)
- worthy of comparison (Romans 8:18)
- a situation in Jerusalem worthy of a visit from Paul (1 Corinthians 16:4)
- Thessalonians' faith worthy of Paul's thanks (2 Thessalonians 1:3)
- a statement worthy of acceptance (1 Timothy 1:15, 4:9)
- world not worthy of the saints (Hebrews 11:38)

Although God's grace is a free gift and no one deserves it, the word "worthy" is also applied to the one who humbly accepts this offer from God:

- accepting the apostles' message and showing them hospitality (Matthew 10:11, 13)
- accepting the king's invitation to the great banquet (Matthew 22:8)
- Jews who did not accept the message being unworthy of eternal life (Acts 13:46)
- those in Sardis who had not defiled their garments being worthy to walk with Jesus (Revelation 3:4)

This principle is well demonstrated in the Parable of the Soils. Every soil was presented with the gift or opportunity of receiving the seed. But only the good soil, by nature of its response, produced a lasting blessing. An individual's response shows whether he or she is worthy or not. God's grace brings our attitudes/responses into balance.

3. Some have taken this act of "judging the body" to an extreme of making the Lord's Supper a time for publicly confirming who is a member of the body and who is not (i.e., a sign of fellowship). This is not to say that a congregation of disciples is not responsible in some way for evaluating the spirituality of each member; for instance, in 1 Corinthians 5:1–13 Paul clearly expected the faithful members of the church to publicly judge any unrepentant members: "With such a man do not even eat" and "Expel the wicked man from among you" (vv11, 13). Although this disciplinary action was even to be included in the church's program of assembly when necessary, there is no indication that it was meant to be a part or function of the Lord's Supper. With full knowledge of what was about to happen, Jesus allowed Judas to participate in the first celebration of the Lord's Supper, and Judas "ate and drank judgment on himself" through his unworthy participation.

4. *Merriam Webster's Collegiate Dictionary,* 10th ed., s.v. "judgment."

5. Since the Greek language allows the metaphor of "fallen asleep" to mean "physical death" (as in 1 Corinthians 15:6), many commentators hold that the judgment (condemnation) being discussed here involved literal sickness and death. This is not impossible when one considers the judgment of God on Ananias and Sapphira in Acts 5:1–11. However, this writer prefers a more allegorical interpretation, hearkening back to the night when Jesus was betrayed (1 Corinthians 11:23), and how the overconfident disciples demonstrated their *weakness* and *powerlessness* by *falling asleep.* Although this happened on the physical plane, there are clear spiritual implications: the disciples of Jesus were spiritually weak and sick, and had even fallen asleep.

10

From Simplicity to Ceremony

Although the interval between the beginning of the church in Jerusalem and the completion of the last New Testament letter was probably somewhere between forty and sixty-five years, there is no indication that the celebration of the Lord's Supper was modified in any way during that time.[1] Almost twenty-five years after its first celebration, Paul clearly taught that this unpretentious remembrance, which was originally celebrated in the homes of disciples, should retain its simplicity—even when it moved into the larger, more public assemblies of the church (1 Corinthians 11:17–34). Sadly, the same worldly thinking that assailed first century Judaism also attacked the practice of Christianity, and although most of the New Testament letters enjoyed a wide circulation among believers in the first century, man-made traditions and humanistic thinking soon began to have an effect on their interpretation.

It is truly amazing to think that Jesus' simple presentation of the bread and the cup during the Last Supper could ever have evolved into the elaborate programs presently observed by many Christian denominations. The rules and regulations governing these modern-day celebrations rival and in some cases exceed the pomp, procedure and ceremony of the Old Testament Passover. The memorial meal that was shared so humbly in an upper room by the Lord and his closest disciples for the purpose of attuning their hearts to his suffering and sacrifice, has become for many a ritual that not only borders on mysticism (receiving spiritual truth or power through subjective experience) but reinforces the man-made division between clergy and laity. For many, the simplicity of the Lord's Supper has been lost amid a complex construction of human authority, man-made tradition and elaborate ceremony.

Real Presence

When we review the trends and developments in Christian tradition through the centuries following the New Testament period, we can see that the doctrine that most starkly embodies a significant shift in the understanding and practice of the Lord's Supper is what is known as the "Real Presence." This teaching asserts that "Jesus is literally and wholly present in the Holy Eucharist—body and blood, soul and divinity—under the appearances of bread and wine."[2] The implications of such an understanding are immense: every time the Lord's Supper is celebrated, the body and blood of Jesus are literally sacrificed again. And through the ingestion of the consecrated bread and wine, participants assimilate the physical body and blood of Jesus into their organic bodies, as well as his soul and divinity into their spiritual being. This doctrine has become one of the central dogmas of both the Roman Catholic and Orthodox faiths. Considering the influence that these two groups have had on Christian thought, it is imperative to understand the origins of this doctrine and how it relates to the teaching of the New Testament.

As discussed earlier in chapter 5, Jesus' use of metaphor in John 6 concerning the eating of his flesh and drinking of his blood was totally in line with his use of metaphor in earlier chapters of that same Gospel. Just as Nicodemus inquired if being born again meant that he had to physically enter into his mother's womb for a second time (John 3), and the woman at the well wondered how Jesus would get living water out of the well without a rope and a bucket (John 4), the crowd in John 6 took offense at Jesus' words, thinking he was literally challenging them to eat his flesh and drink his blood. The overly literal interpretations of Nicodemus, the woman at the well and the crowd in John 6 were all incorrect—Jesus was speaking figuratively of spiritual truths. Although John 6 is predominantly used as the beginning point of the "transubstantiation" argument, it is interesting to note that these two earlier metaphors actually describe the New Testament teaching on the "real presence" of Jesus in the hearts of his disciples. Jesus taught that one must be born of water and the Spirit to enter the kingdom of God (John 3) and that the living water he was able to give would become a spring of water welling up to eternal life and causing a person to never thirst again (John 4). The metaphor of "living water" was further explained in John 7:37–39:

> On the last and greatest day of the Feast, Jesus stood and said in a loud voice, "If anyone is thirsty, let him come to me and drink. Whoever believes in me, as the Scripture has said, streams of living water will flow from within him." By this he meant the Spirit, whom those who believed in him were later to receive. Up to that time the Spirit had not been given, since Jesus had not yet been glorified.

Receiving the Spirit marks one's initiation into the kingdom of God, and continuously being filled with the Spirit marks one's membership. Peter equated this spiritual rebirth with baptism in Acts 2:38, wherein he proclaimed God's promise: "Repent and be baptized, every one of you, in the name of Jesus Christ for the forgiveness of your sins; and you will receive the gift of the Holy Spirit."

The correct response of faith to the message of the gospel is repentance and baptism. Other passages demonstrate that at the moment of baptism a believer receives the indwelling Spirit of God through faith and thereby receives new life:

> We were therefore buried with him through baptism into death in order that, just as Christ was raised from the dead through the glory of the Father, we too may live a new life. (Romans 6:4)

> And you were also included in Christ when you heard the word of truth, the gospel of your salvation. Having believed, you were marked in him with a seal, the promised Holy Spirit, who is a deposit guaranteeing our inheritance until

> the redemption of those who are God's possession to the praise of his glory. (Ephesians 1:13)

> I have become its [the church's] servant by the commission God gave me to present to you the word of God in its fullness—the mystery that has been kept hidden for ages and generations, but is now disclosed to the saints. To them God has chosen to make known among the Gentiles the glorious riches of this mystery, which is Christ in you, the hope of glory. (Colossians 1:25–27)

> And if anyone does not have the Spirit of Christ, he does not belong to Christ. But if Christ is in you, your body is dead because of sin, yet your spirit is alive because of righteousness. And if the Spirit of him who raised Jesus from the dead is living in you, he who raised Christ from the dead will also give life to your mortal bodies through his Spirit, who lives in you. (Romans 8:9b–11)

Once someone has received the gift of the Holy Spirit through baptism, Jesus lives in that person by his Spirit. This is the real presence of Christ that Jesus promised to his disciples. This truth alone makes redundant and contradictory all other arguments for the ongoing need for the bread and the wine to literally impart the presence of Christ.

> Now it is God who makes both us and you stand firm in Christ. He anointed us, set his seal of ownership on us, and put his Spirit in our hearts as a deposit, guaranteeing what is to come. (2 Corinthians 1:21–22)

The problem with the supposed miracle of transubstantiation is *not* that it would be impossible for God to accomplish this, but that there is no scriptural basis or need that warrants it. A person who has already received the gift of the indwelling Holy Spirit does not need to continually receive that gift again and again. This reception of God's Spirit as a deposit is a one-time event accompanying spiritual rebirth.[3] Although it never needs to be repeated, we often need to be reminded of the incredible gift that God has given us: Christ living in us.

> Do you not know that your body is a temple of the Holy Spirit, who is in you, whom you have received from God? You are not your own; you were bought at a price. Therefore honor God with your body. (1 Corinthians 6:19–20)

The dangerous and erroneous implication of the doctrine of the Real Presence in the Eucharist is that the real presence that believers already possess after receiving the gift of the Holy Spirit in their hearts is somehow inadequate or deteriorates over time. Nothing could be further from the truth—he "has given us the Spirit in our hearts as a deposit, guaranteeing what is to come" (2 Corinthians 5:5).

True Sacrifice

The New Testament not only fails to support the doctrine of Real Presence of Christ in the Eucharist in terms of purpose and function, but also fails to supply a basis for the idea that the Lord's Supper was ever meant to be understood as a literal sacrifice of the body and blood of Jesus. *The Catholic Encyclopedia* states:

> If the Mass is to be a true sacrifice in the literal sense, it must realize the philosophical conception of sacrifice.... According to the comparative history of religions, four things are necessary to a sacrifice:
> - a sacrificial gift (*res oblata*),
> - a sacrificing minister (*minister legitimus*),
> - a sacrificial action (*actio sacrificica*), and
> - a sacrificial end or object (*finis sacrificii*).[4]

Therefore, if the Eucharistic Sacrifice of the Mass is truly a foundational concept, then the inspired witness of the New Testament Scriptures should clearly show the existence of these four necessary components in relation to the celebration of the Lord's Supper: the sacrificial gift, the sacrificial minister, the sacrificial action and the sacrificial objective.

When applied to the required sacrifices of the Old Testament law and to the personal sacrifice of Jesus Christ, the New Testament confirms the validity of such a model. The work of the high priest in the Old Testament is described in these words:

> Every high priest is selected from among men and is appointed to represent them in matters related to God, to offer gifts and sacrifices for sins. He is able to deal gently with those who are ignorant and are going astray, since he himself is subject to weakness. This is why he has to offer sacrifices for his own sins, as well as for the sins of the people. No one takes this honor upon himself; he must be called by God, just as Aaron was. (Hebrews 5:1–4)

All four components are easily identifiable: the high priest (a sacrificing minister) offers (sacrificial action) gifts and sacrifices (sacrificial gifts) for sins (sacrificial objective). A similar analysis could be made for the ordinary Levitical priests, although their sacrifices were revealed in the New Testament to be incapable of taking away sins:

> Day after day every priest stands and performs his religious duties; again and again he offers the same sacrifices, which can never take away sins. (Hebrews 10:11)

The redemptive work of Jesus is described in the following verse:

> But when this priest [Jesus] had offered for all time one sacrifice for sins, he sat down at the right hand of God. (Hebrews 10:12)

Again, all four components are easily identifiable: Jesus (a sacrificing minister) offered (sacrificial action) one sacrifice (sacrificial gift) for sins (sacrificial objective). The consistency of this model is further underscored by the fact that all of the key words—"priest," "sacrifice" and "to offer"—are translated from the same Greek words in all three examples.

Now when we apply this model to all the instances of the Lord's Supper recorded in the New Testament, we come up with a shocking result:

- the bread and/or the wine of the Lord's Supper are *never* referred to as a "sacrifice";

- the person presiding at the Lord's Supper is *never* referred to as a "priest," and there is no indication whatsoever of mandatory ordination to legitimate the Supper;
- the action of presenting the bread and/or the cup is *never* described as being "offered";
- and finally, the clear words of Jesus that describe the objective of partaking in the Lord's Supper are simply: "Do this in remembrance of me" (Luke 22:19; 1 Corinthians 11:24, 25).

Considering all of these deficiencies and the fact that the New Testament writers were obviously familiar with the appropriate terminology for describing a true sacrifice, we can conclude that the New Testament church did not consider the celebration of the Lord's Supper as a literal sacrifice of the body and blood of Jesus. It was meant as a remembrance and nothing more.

On the other hand, although the New Testament never defines the Lord's Supper as a literal sacrifice, there still remains an undeniable concept of priesthood and sacrifice that is applied to all those who are called by God into his kingdom:

> To him who loves us and has freed us from our sins by his blood, and has made us to be a kingdom and priests to serve his God and Father—to him be glory and power for ever and ever! Amen. (Revelation 1:5–6)

> As you come to him, the living Stone—rejected by men but chosen by God and precious to him—you also, like living stones, are being built into a spiritual house to be a holy priesthood, offering spiritual sacrifices acceptable to God through Jesus Christ. (1 Peter 2:4–5)

Every Christian has been chosen to offer spiritual sacrifices acceptable to God. These sacrifices are specifically defined as our own bodies (Romans 12:1), material help (Philippians 4:18), praise to God (Hebrews 13:15), good deeds (Hebrews 13:16) and sharing with others (Hebrews 13:16). The sacrificial objective of these sacrifices is also stated: "with such sacrifices God is pleased" (Hebrews 13:16).

Once Is Enough

In further opposition to the notion that the Lord's Supper was to be a continual repetition of Christ's physical sacrifice, the New Testament teaches that the sacrifice of Jesus was perfect and that he only needed to offer himself once for all time:

> It was necessary, then, for the copies of the heavenly things to be purified with these sacrifices, but the heavenly things themselves with better sacrifices than these. For Christ did not enter a man-made sanctuary that was only a copy of the true one; he entered heaven itself, now to appear for us in God's presence. Nor did he enter heaven to offer himself again and again, the way the high priest enters the Most Holy Place every year with blood that is not his own. Then Christ would have had to suffer many times since the creation of the world. But now he has appeared once for all at the end of the ages to do away with sin by the sacrifice of himself. Just as man is destined to die once, and after that to face judgment, so Christ was sacrificed once to take away the sins of many people; and he will appear a second time, not to bear sin, but to bring salvation to those who are waiting for him. (Hebrews 9:23–28)

> But when this priest had offered for all time one sacrifice for sins, he sat down at the right hand of God. Since that time he waits for his enemies to be made his footstool, because by one sacrifice he has made perfect forever those who are being made holy. (Hebrews 10:12–14)

Although comparative history of religion tells us that sacrificial systems are not unique to the Bible, no other religion has ever claimed that a single sacrifice was so absolute and powerful that it provided salvation for all people. The effect of Christ's sacrifice is so complete that the Hebrew writer went on to say, "And where these have been forgiven, there is no longer any sacrifice for sin" (Hebrews 10:18). The death of Jesus abolished the need for further sacrifice for sin because the requirements of God were fully met in the offering of his perfect life.

From Presbyters to Priests

While these considerations are sufficient to demonstrate the influence of human tradition on the celebration of the Lord's Supper, let us examine for a moment the origins of the ecclesiastical priesthood as found in the Roman Catholic and Orthodox churches. *The Catholic Encyclopedia* states:

> The proof of the Divine origin of the Catholic priesthood must be regarded as established, once it is shown the Eucharistic Sacrifice of the Mass is coeval [of equal age] with the beginning and the essence of Christianity.[5]

Since we have already shown that the New Testament writers never viewed the bread and the fruit of the vine of the Lord's Supper as a literal sacrifice, the divine origin of the Catholic priesthood must be questioned. At some point in the second century, the idea began to develop that those who served the church in certain leadership roles were in fact a special priesthood—separate from the common people. One of the most significant proofs that this development was not an original concept of the early church is the linguistic evolution of the Greek word *presbuteros* ("elder") that was adopted into the Latin language and eventually gave birth to our modern English word "priest." Consider the following two entries from the *Merriam Webster's Collegiate Dictionary:*

- **priest** \prēst\ *noun* [Middle English *preist,* from Old English *prēost,* ultimately from Late Latin *presbyter* — more at PRESBYTER] (before twelfth century):
  one authorized to perform the sacred rites of a religion, especially as a mediatory agent between humans and God; specifically: an Anglican, Eastern Orthodox, or Roman Catholic clergyman ranking below a bishop and above a deacon
- **pres·by·ter** \ prez-bə-tər , pres- \ *noun* [Late Latin, elder, priest, from Greek *presbyteros,* comparative of *presbys* old man, elder; akin to Greek *pro* before and Greek *bainein* to go —more at FOR, COME] (1597)

1: a member of the governing body of an early Christian church

2: a member of the order of priests in churches having episcopal hierarchies that include bishops, priests, and deacons

3: ELDER

The Greek language of the New Testament clearly delineated between the words "priest" and "elder" since the two were very distinct roles in the Jewish community (mentioned together sixty-two times in the Bible). The term "elder" was also adopted by the apostles and used to designate those men who were selected to lead locally in congregations of the New Testament church (Jerusalem—Acts 11:30; 15:2, 4, 6, 22, 23; 16:4; 21:18; Lystra, Iconium and Antioch—Acts 14:23; Ephesus—Acts 20:17; cities of Crete—Titus 1:5). At some point after the completion of the New Testament, the meaning of the word "elder" began to weaken. In time the concept of priest became so embedded in the word *presbuteros* that the word was adopted into the Latin language and became synonymous with the Latin word for "priest" (*sacerdos*). The fact that this word was *transliterated* into Latin as opposed to being *translated* proves that its common usage had already deviated from its original meaning, so a direct translation would have caused confusion for those already using the word. Any attempt to prove the existence of priesthood in the New Testament church based on the presence of the word *presbuteros* is unfounded and illogical. The word was corrupted by misuse and undisputedly meant "elder" in the New Testament text without a trace of the meaning of "priest."

Although the word *presbuteros* was never synonymous with "priest" in the New Testament, it was used interchangeably with another word that is worthy of mention—*episkopos*, meaning "bishop" or "overseer." This word is only used five times in the New Testament, and in two instances it is specifically used together with "elder":

> From Miletus, Paul sent to Ephesus for the elders of the church. When they arrived, he said to them... "Keep watch

over yourselves and all the flock of which the Holy Spirit has made you *overseers*." (Acts 20:17, 18, 28, emphasis mine)

The reason I left you in Crete was that you might straighten out what was left unfinished and appoint elders in every town. An elder must be blameless, the husband of but one wife, a man whose children believe and are not open to the charge of being wild and disobedient. Since an *overseer* is entrusted with God's work, he must be blameless—not overbearing, not quick-tempered, not given to drunkenness, not violent, not pursuing dishonest gain. (Titus 1:5–7, emphasis mine)

As the preceding dictionary definitions explain, the Anglican, Roman Catholic and Eastern Orthodox churches maintain a hierarchy that places "bishops" over "priests," and yet the New Testament uses the terms "bishop" and "presbyter" to describe the same role and therefore the same level of leadership. Also of note is the requirement that elders/bishops must be married and have believing children (see also 1 Timothy 3:1–7). In direct contradiction to this mandate of God through the apostle Paul, the Roman Catholic and Orthodox churches forbid the bishop to marry, and the Roman Catholic Church goes even further to forbid priests to marry as well. In the chapter that follows Paul's command that bishops "must be...the husband of but one wife" (1 Timothy 3:2), he gives this warning:

The Spirit clearly says that in later times some will abandon the faith and follow deceiving spirits and things taught by demons. Such teachings come through hypocritical liars, whose consciences have been seared as with a hot iron. They forbid people to marry and order them to abstain from certain foods, which God created to be received with thanksgiving by those who believe and who know the truth. (1 Timothy 4:1–3)

In direct opposition to the teaching of the Bible and in frightful fulfillment of a New Testament prophecy,[6] the Roman Catholic and Orthodox traditions forbid the "bishop" to marry. Therefore, the ecclesiastical priesthood as practiced by the Roman Catholic and Orthodox churches is not Biblical—in fact, according to the apostle Paul, it is an abandonment of the faith and a following of deceiving spirits and things taught by demons. In addition, the Roman Catholic Church teaches that the bread of the Lord's Supper represents both the body and the blood of Jesus, and from the late twelfth century until recent times, reserved the right to drink the fruit of the vine almost exclusively for the clergy. Therefore, even the second part of Paul's prophecy is fulfilled by Roman Catholic tradition—"they order them to abstain from certain foods, which God created to be received with thanksgiving by those who believe and who know the truth." Although Jesus asked his disciples to eat the bread and drink the cup, Roman Catholic tradition forbade the majority of her members to drink the cup for centuries. Certain "Christians" of our day are repeating the same mistakes that were made by the certain Jews of Jesus' day: God's word is ignored and the traditions of men are being followed. Jesus' challenge to the Pharisees still rings out:

> "And why do you break the command of God for the sake of your tradition?…Thus you nullify the word of God for the sake of your tradition. You hypocrites! Isaiah was right when he prophesied about you:
>
>> "'These people honor me with their lips,
>>> but their hearts are far from me.
>> They worship me in vain;
>>> their teachings are but rules taught by men.'"
>
> (Matthew 15:3,6–9; including a quote from Isaiah 29:13)

When man-made religious teachings are given more respect and authority than the word of God, following traditions becomes sinful and wrong. There are many more human traditions surrounding the celebration of the Lord's Supper, such as the construction of a physical altar and sanctuary, mandatory fasting before reception, etc., but these teachings only serve to reinforce the false doctrines of the "literal sacrifice," the Real Presence in the Eucharist and the separation of clergy and laity.

Both the history of Israel and two thousand years of church history illustrate that man is often not satisfied to only follow God's word. As time passes, people often feel the need for something different (2 Timothy 4:3). They often want something more impressive. Leaders frequently want something that enhances their position or their authority. Unlike the Judaism from which it sprang, Christianity has few ceremonies and rituals. As the one regularly celebrated event, the Lord's Supper became the most apparent activity to be developed by those wanting more mystery, awe and gravity, as well as something that would strengthen the control that leaders had over their people. Such political and humanistic thinking has transformed the most simple of remembrances into a complex ritual, weighed down with rules and regulations.

Summary

Although God used Moses to guide the Israelites through a number of transitions with regard to the celebration of the Passover, the New Testament gives no indication that the Lord's Supper was to evolve in a similar manner. During the twenty-five year span between Jesus' institution of the Supper and the writing of Paul's corrective teaching to the Corinthians, there do not appear to have been any changes. And nowhere else in the New Testament were such changes ever mentioned or alluded to.

In contrast to the simplicity of the early church's practices, the oldest Christian denominations have added elaborate liturgy and ceremony to the celebration of the Lord's Supper. It is not possible to trace with exactness how all these changes came about, but suffice it to say a number of errant doctrines have developed and solidified, deviating more and more from the practices of the New Testament. Among these doctrines are the "Real Presence of Christ in the Eucharist", the "Eucharistic Sacrifice" and the "Sacrament of Priesthood." These doctrines are so mutually dependent that either they must all be true or they are all false. By examining the theological assumptions behind each of these doctrines, their danger becomes clear since they fundamentally contradict the inspired teaching of the New Testament.

- The New Testament teaches that one can receive the gift of the indwelling Holy Spirit through spiritual rebirth. This gift is a deposit guaranteeing what is to come; but the doctrine of the Real Presence of Christ in the Eucharist implies that there is something more to receive, and therefore, this deposit is not sufficient.
- The New Testament teaches that Jesus offered himself once for all time as the one sacrifice for sins; but the doctrine of the Eucharistic Sacrifice implies that this was not enough and that the body and blood of Jesus must be perpetually offered until his return.
- The New Testament teaches that all believers are priests before God and never mentions a separate earthly priesthood in the church; but the Sacrament of Priesthood disagrees with the Scriptures and establishes a human, physical priesthood.

Of course, many of these doctrines go even further. Celibacy became a requirement for holding the office of bishop, and the common members of the Roman Catholic Church were not allowed to drink the cup of the Lord's Supper. Such stipulations directly violate Paul's requirement that the bishop be married and Jesus' command that all disciples should remember him through eating the bread and drinking the cup. Like the Pharisees of Jesus' day, these denominations "break the command of God for the sake of [their] tradition" (Matthew 15:3). What God has made simple, let no man complicate!

Notes

1. With the possible exception of a shift from the context of a full *agape* meal.

2. http://www.catholic.com/library/Real_Presence.asp

3. Certainly there are passages that talk about *Christians* being "filled with the Holy Spirit" time and again. Acts 4:8, 31; 13:9, 52, for example, refer to an increased fervency of spiritual activity and devotion to the Lord. Ephesians 5:18 is simply an enjoinder to be spiritually minded.

4. *The Catholic Encyclopedia,* at http://www.newadvent.org/cathen/10006a.htm, s.v. "Sacrifice of the Mass."

5. *The Catholic Encyclopedia,* at http://www.newadvent.org/cathen/12409a.htm, s.v. "Priesthood."

6. In the original context, Paul was probably referring to certain Gnostic-type groups with ascetic tendencies. However, his warnings apply only too well to certain practices in the Roman Catholic and Orthodox churches.

Epilogue

This book was not a book that I planned to write. It evolved out of a series of lessons I prepared on the meaning and celebration of the Lord's Supper while leading a church in Moscow. As noted in the introduction to this book, it is almost impossible for an observer of history *not* to be influenced by his or her own particular situation and context. This definitely includes me. In July of 1991, just weeks before the infamous coup that initiated the breakup of the Soviet Union, my wife, Tammy, and I, with our baby daughter, Britain, in tow, moved to Moscow, Russia, with a team of fifteen other people. In addition to another ministry couple who led the church planting for the first three weeks, the team included nine college students and four former Soviet and Eastern bloc citizens who had been converted in our congregations beyond the borders of the USSR. Considering that only three of the Americans spoke Russian (one fluently and two others had finished one year of university study), that four of the team members had been believers for less than eight months, and that only four of us had had any significant ministry experience—everything that was about to happen can only be attributed to faith, prayer, God's word and his miraculous power.

The 'Early Church'—Moscow Style

After just five days of sharing our faith on the streets, we held the first service of the church in Moscow on July 14 with 268 in attendance. From that very first meeting, the Lord added daily to our number those who were being saved (Acts 2:42) and during the next twelve months we saw 850 people baptized into Christ. Although it had been our practice in other places to celebrate the Lord's Supper during our public Sunday worship service, the sheer numbers of visitors initially made this impractical. Instead, after our regular worship service, comprised of singing, praying, testimony and preaching, we would have about an hour of fellowship before we would gather the members back together again. At this much smaller meeting, usually accompanied by some of the more eager visitors, the disciples would celebrate the Lord's Supper in small groups there in our rented hall or else in nearby parks. I will never forget taking a small group to the park right under the Kremlin wall in early September of 1991 and breaking bread and sharing the fruit of the vine together. Soldiers stood nearby at their stations, Muscovites were strolling in the afternoon sun, and there in a little corner garden of the park, disciples of Jesus circled together singing softly and thanking God in prayer—remembering the incredible sacrifice of Jesus Christ.

By January of 1992, winter conditions, combined with economic recession due to the collapse of the USSR, moved us into another pattern. After our regular Sunday service we would go back to our apartments, scattered throughout Moscow, for a fellowship meal of soup and bread, followed by the Lord's Supper. For many of our poorer members, these meals not only provided a time of awesome fellowship, but also actually satisfied a true physical need. Among all my memories of our eight years of ministry in Moscow, these house church meetings are among some of the most dear and vivid. With twenty or so people jammed into our small living room and half the people seated on the floor, we first shared our soup and bread together, and then remembered Jesus in the Lord's Supper. It was awesome!

Although the food situation improved somewhat by early May of 1992, we were now facing another problem—the church was approaching five hundred members, and we no longer had access to enough apartments. The few apartments where the team members were living were already being used multiple times each Sunday; and two-thirds of the church membership was teens and college students who either lived at home with their families or in small dorm rooms on campus. Also, by this time we had moved into an incredible new venue called the Palace of Youth, constructed during the previous decade by visionaries in the Communist Youth Party. This facility, which included an 1,850-seat auditorium, became operational just months before the Soviet Union disintegrated and never managed to become connected with any established government program—so it became the home of our church for the next few years! Since we were not allowed to take food into the auditorium at this time, we went back to celebrating the Lord's Supper in small groups after our worship service in the reception foyer of the Palace—which was almost as big as the auditorium itself. At times the administration would allow us to bring blankets and food, and reminiscent of Jesus and the feeding of the multitudes, we would sit on the floor in small groups of the foyer to eat, and then celebrate the Lord's Supper together. This pattern continued for about eighteen months. Then, in the fall of 1993, we outgrew the Palace of Youth and moved into regional facilities such as movie theaters and union halls in different parts of the city. We adapted once again and introduced the more familiar (to Americans) trays for the bread and individual cups for the fruit of the vine and have continued celebrating in this manner until now.

I believe this history is important for a number of reasons. Our constantly changing circumstances forced us to keep reevaluating our effectiveness in celebrating the Lord's Supper. Also, every disciple developed an intuitive connection between the Lord's Supper and the fellowship of their Christian family. Finally, the emphasis given to celebrating the Lord's Supper helped cultivate a deeper spirituality in an "unversed" (Biblically speaking) population. From this base of disciples in Moscow, we planted another twenty-three churches in the remaining former Soviet Republics, as well as taking responsibility for a twenty-fifth church in Mongolia. By the time we left Moscow in 1999, the combined membership of all of these churches was more than 9,500 people and every one of these churches was being led by nationals. These original disciples in Moscow accomplished so much more than I or any other human being could take any credit for. And I firmly believe it was through their convictions and personal relationships with God that this incredible growth became a reality. In the two and a half years since our departure, seven new congregations have been planted and the membership has increased by more than 2,000 disciples. Circumstances that initially appeared difficult and negative were transformed into incredible blessings by God's power. As I celebrate the Lord's Supper today, I remember not only the body of our Lord on the cross, but also the body of Christ of which I am a member and the precious relationships with brothers and sisters all over the world.

Proclamation of His Death

The effects of the Protestant Reformation on Christian thought in the Western world cannot be overstated. As a result, many of us are very sensitive to the rituals and traditionalism often present in the Roman Catholic and Orthodox faiths. For this reason, there is much more danger, in my opinion, of falling for the secularism of the Sadducees than of creating more rules and regulations like the Pharisees did. Jesus condemned the Sadducees because they did "not know the Scriptures or the power of God" (Matthew 22:29). We need to be reminded that Jesus gave up equality with God and lived in a physical body just like we do (Philippians 2:5–8). And what is more, Jesus was tempted in every way just as we are, although he never sinned (Hebrews 4:15), and then willingly offered his life (John 10:17–18) as the perfect sacrifice for our sins (Hebrews 9:26). To expect society at large to support or even to accept our faith is both erroneous and naive, since Satan is continuously working through this material world to distract our minds, discourage our hearts and destroy our hope.

Although we have been given incredible freedom to create the atmosphere of celebration surrounding the Lord's Supper, using any combination of acceptable elements of worship (such as singing, preaching, Scripture reading, prayer, teaching, exhortation, testimony, etc.), we must be careful that the end result always fulfills the command of Jesus: "Do this in remembrance of me." In today's world as much as ever, the regular celebration of the Lord's Supper is vital to the strengthening of our faith in the resurrection of Jesus Christ: "For whenever you eat this bread and drink this cup, you proclaim the Lord's death until he comes" (1 Corinthians 11:26). We should never let the presence of visitors among us dampen our proclamation of Christ's death and resurrection or quench our admission of our sinfulness that caused his death to take place; the glory must go to God. This common proclamation of faith is first and foremost for each other, but it can also have an incredible effect on those visiting:

> But if an unbeliever or someone who does not understand comes in while everybody is prophesying, he will be convinced by all that he is a sinner and will be judged by all, and the secrets of his heart will be laid bare. So he will fall down and worship God, exclaiming, "God is really among you!" (1 Corinthians 14:24–25)

Of course, the strength of the Lord's Supper is simply the message of the cross as Paul so powerfully declared:

> I am not ashamed of the gospel, because it is the power of God for the salvation of everyone who believes: first for the Jew, then for the Gentile. For in the gospel a righteousness from God is revealed, a righteousness that is by faith from first to last, just as it is written: "The righteous will live by faith." (Romans 1:16, 17)

> For the message of the cross is foolishness to those who are perishing, but to us who are being saved it is the power of God. For it is written: "I will destroy the wisdom of the wise; the intelligence of the intelligent I will frustrate." Where is the wise man? Where is the scholar? Where is the philosopher of this age? Has not God made foolish the wisdom of the world? For since in the wisdom of God the world through its wisdom did not know him, God was pleased through the foolishness of what was preached to save those who

> believe. Jews demand miraculous signs and Greeks look for wisdom, but we preach Christ crucified: a stumbling block to Jews and foolishness to Gentiles, but to those whom God has called, both Jews and Greeks, Christ the power of God and the wisdom of God. For the foolishness of God is wiser than man's wisdom, and the weakness of God is stronger than man's strength. (1 Corinthians 1:18–25)

To those looking for human wisdom or miraculous signs, the Lord's Supper is indeed foolishness. But to those who have put their faith in Christ as "the power of God and wisdom of God," it is a poignant reminder of the most amazing message ever preached:

> For what I received I passed on to you as of first importance: Christ died for our sins according to the Scriptures, that he was buried, that he was raised on the third day according to the Scriptures. (1 Corinthians 15:3–4)

The gospel has not changed in two thousand years—it still is the "good news."

Training the Heart

I would like to close by pointing out an additional blessing that is received through the faithful celebration of the Lord's Supper: it trains the hearts of God's people to have devotional time with him on their own. In his letter to the Colossians, Paul struggled for disciples that he had never even met when he learned that they were being assaulted by all kinds of humanistic teaching:

> My purpose is that they may be encouraged in heart and united in love, so that they may have the full riches of complete understanding, in order that they may know the mystery of God, namely, Christ, in whom are hidden all the treasures of wisdom and knowledge. I tell you this so that no one may deceive you by fine-sounding arguments. (Colossians 2:2–4)

The celebration of the Lord's Supper is a constant reminder that we have not put our faith in man's strength or human philosophy, but in a loving God who was willing to sacrifice his precious Son to redeem our souls from death. The tone we set in our celebrations of the Lord's Supper has a great effect on the tone of our Christian lives—whether for good or bad: "That is why many among you are weak and sick, and a number of you have fallen asleep" (1 Corinthians 11:30). If we treat the Lord's Supper lightly and avoid taking the time to reflect deeply on the sacrifice of Jesus, we are setting a precedent for superficial quiet times (daily personal devotionals) and weak spirituality.[1]

To the very end of his natural life on earth, Jesus demonstrated his humility and obedience to God through service and love for his disciples, and by offering his life as a sacrifice for many. The disciples now believed what Jesus had known all along: "Blessed is the man who perseveres under trial, because when he has stood the test, he will receive the crown of life that God has promised to those who love him" (James 1:12). Today we stand in need of this remembrance as much as our brothers and sisters of the first century.

> For our struggle is not against flesh and blood, but against the rulers, against the authorities, against the powers of this dark world and against the spiritual forces of evil in the heavenly realms. (Ephesians 6:12)

Satan fights to take away God's word that is sown in our hearts. Trouble or persecution tests the depth of our convictions and tries to wither our faith in God's word. The "worries of this life...the deceitfulness of wealth and the desires for other things" (Mark 4:19) compete with God's word for the resources of our hearts and threaten us with unfruitfulness and unproductiveness. We desperately need to meditate on the heart and sacrifice of Jesus Christ—we need to sit at his table of fellowship and participate in his body and in his blood. Whether gathered together with the whole church in public assembly, or with just a few disciples in a private room or a place of prayer, Jesus calls us to his table for fellowship with him and each other. Sharing the bread and the fruit of the vine together strengthens our resolve to fight the good fight and hold on to faith and a good conscience. Across the centuries and continents, despite persecution and opposition from within and without, and through struggles and hardships in every generation, the Lord's death must be proclaimed until he comes. Let us honor and obey this request of our Lord and Savior Jesus Christ: *"Do this in remembrance of me."*

Note

1. The fact that some congregations presently combine the prayers for the bread and for the fruit of the vine and then virtually pass them at the same time, may reflect a desire to expedite this part of the worship service just a little too quickly. There is nothing more motivating or life changing than reflection on the incredible sacrifice of Jesus Christ; we need to take the time to proclaim it effectively.

Appendix 1

A Chronological Narrative of the Lord's Supper

	Summary of Events	Matthew	Mark	Luke	John
1.	Jesus knows that his time has come.				13:1
2.	Two disciples (Mark), Peter and John (Luke), prepare the Passover.	26:17–19	14:12–16	22:7–13	13:1
3.	Jesus reclines with his disciples.	26:20	14:17–18	22:14	
4.	Jesus takes the cup, gives thanks and says that he will not drink it again until the kingdom of God comes.			22:15–18	
5.	The devil had already prompted Judas Iscariot to betray Jesus.				13:2
6.	Jesus predicts his betrayal. The disciples ask, "Surely not I, Lord?" —Judas singles himself out by saying, "Rabbi" and not "Lord" (Matthew).	26:21–25	14:18–21		
7.	Jesus institutes the Lord's Supper.	26:26–29	14:22–25	22:19–20	
8.	Jesus predicts his betrayal (second time). The disciples ask among themselves who it might be. A dispute arises among the disciples as to who is the greatest.			22:21–23 22:24	
9.	Jesus washes the disciples' feet.				13:2–11
10.	Jesus teaches that the greatest should be the servant, like him.			22:25–27	13:12–17
11.	Jesus predicts his betrayal (third time) and gives Judas a piece of bread as a sign. Judas leaves, but the disciples do not understand. Jesus explains that it is time for the Son of Man to be glorified and that he is going away.				13:18–30 13:31–36
12.	Jesus promises to give the kingdom to his disciples.			22:28–30	
13.	Jesus specifically warns Peter about his denial. Peter protests.			22:31–34	13:37–38

	Summary of Events	Matthew	Mark	Luke	John
14.	Jesus teaches about heaven, his revelation of the Father, the coming of the Spirit of truth and the Spirit's future indwelling of the faithful.				14:1–31
15.	Jesus prepares his disciples to be sent out again—this time with purse and bag, and even swords.			22:35–38	
16.	They sing a hymn and go out to the Mount of Olives.	26:30	14:26	22:39	14:31
17.	Jesus teaches them the Parable of the Vine and the Branches.				15:1–17
	Jesus warns them about the world hating them as it has hated him.				15:18–16:4
	Jesus teaches that he must leave so that the Spirit can come.				16:5–16
	Jesus teaches that he must return to the Father so that they will also have a direct relationship with the Father.				16:17–31
18.	Jesus predicts the scattering of the disciples, their reunion in Galilee and his victory over the world (John).	26:31–32	14:27–28		16:32–33
19.	Peter protests, and Jesus predicts his denial. Peter disagrees, and the others say the same.	26:33–35	14:29–31		
20.	Jesus prays for himself, for his disciples and for all future believers.				17:1–26
21.	Jesus prays in Gethsemane, where an angel ministers to him. He sweats drops of blood (Luke) and the disciples sleep.	26:36–46	14:32–42	22:40–46	18:1
22.	Judas leads an armed crowd to Jesus and betrays him with a kiss.	26:47–50	14:43–46	22:47–48	18:2–9
23.	Peter (John) cuts off a servant's ear with a sword, but Jesus heals it (Luke).	26:51–54	14:47	22:49–51	18:10–11
24.	Jesus surrenders, and the disciples desert him.	26:55–56	14:48–50	22:51–53	18:12

Appendix 2

A Conflated Narrative of the Lord's Supper

Matthew 26:26–29, Mark 14:22–25, Luke 22:18–20

Matthew, Mark, Luke	Matthew, Mark	Matthew, Luke	Mark, Luke	Matthew	Mark	Luke
						And
	while they were eating {Jesus}					
						{he}
took bread, gave thanks and broke it, and gave it to						
	{his disciples}					{them}
saying,						
	"Take					
					it;	
				and eat;		
this is my body						
						given for you; do this in remembrance of me."
	Then					
						In the same way, after the supper,
he took the cup,						
	gave thanks and offered it to them,					
		saying,				
				"Drink from it, all of you."		

Matthew, Mark, Luke	Matthew, Mark	Matthew, Luke	Mark, Luke	Matthew	Mark	Luke
					And they all drank from it.	
	{"This is my blood of the [new]* covenant,}					{"This cup is the new covenant in my blood,}
which is poured out for						
	{many}					{you}
				for the forgiveness of sins."		
					He said to them.	
						"For
I tell you						
					the truth,	
I will not drink						
of			again			
			{the}	{this}		
fruit of the vine						
				from now on		
until						
	{that day when I drink it anew}					{the kingdom of God comes."}
				{with you}		
				{in my Father's kingdom."}	{in the kingdom of God."}	

Notes

* indicates some manuscripts

Where there is an overlap, Matthew is used as the preferred text.

Who Are We?

Discipleship Publications International (DPI) began publishing in 1993. We are a nonprofit Christian publisher affiliated with the International Churches of Christ, committed to publishing and distributing materials that honor God, lift up Jesus Christ and show how his message practically applies to all areas of life. We have a deep conviction that no one changes life like Jesus and that the implementation of his teaching will revolutionize any life, any marriage, any family and any singles household.

Since our beginning, we have published more than 125 titles; plus, we have produced a number of important, spiritual audio products. More than 2 million volumes have been printed, and our works have been translated into more than a dozen languages—international is not just a part of our name! Our books are shipped regularly to every inhabited continent.

To see a more detailed description of our works, find us on the World Wide Web at www.dpibooks.org. You can order books by calling 1-888-DPI-BOOK twenty-four hours a day. From outside the US, call 978-670-8840 during Boston-area business hours.

We appreciate the hundreds of comments we have received from readers. We would love to hear from you. Here are other ways to get in touch:

Mail: DPI, 2 Sterling Road, Billerica, Mass. 01862-2595
E-Mail: dpibooks@icoc.org

Find us on the Web
www.dpibooks.org